# WHAT PEOPLE ARE SAYING

This book gives practical instructions on how anyone can learn to pray and have an intimate relationship with God. Pastor Nora's teaching, not only reveals the benefits of a consistent prayer life, but she has set the example over the years by her lifestyle of prayer. *30 Days to A Better Prayer Life* is straight from the heart of a person that has faced tremendous odds and did not give up. As you read it, I believe you will be motivated and inspired to spend more time in prayer.

Pastor Don Clowers
Grace Church USA
Dallas, Texas

Having known Nora King for thirty-eight years, both as her pastor and a friend, I have been impressed with her growth and commitment to God's Kingdom. Out of her personal and pastoral experiences, Nora brings insight and warmth in these difficult times.

Reverend Tom Everett
Knoxville, Tennessee

Author, Nora King, has discovered ways to gain God's attention in prayer. In this book, she shares principles from God's Word that she has walked in throughout the last three decades. Pastor Nora writes with a freshness and zeal that will inspire the reader to "continue in prayer."

Diane Parsons
Parsons Publishing House

Prayer is probably the greatest opportunity and privilege that we have as human beings. Think about an audience with the Almighty! When we think about the possibilities and opportunities, it is tremendous!

In times of great financial crisis, to have an audience with a wealthy benefactor to state your needs in the hopes of getting help—what an opportunity; to have a health issue and be able to meet with a skilled physician to get him on your case—what a blessing; to need employment and to get an appointment with the owner of the corporation—tremendous! We all know how important the right connection at the right time, can be. How much more can God, our Heavenly Father, do than any human can do? He is the Almighty, the Most High, the all-capable One! Prayer is an adventure with Him. Prayer is not just a labor or drudgery or duty. It truly is a privilege. He can do what no other can.

This book, **30 Days to A Better Prayer Life,** will inspire you, motivate you, and encourage you to have that better prayer life. When we enjoy prayer, fellowshipping with God, all of life becomes better, more exciting and more meaningful. To say the truths in this book will stimulate and inspire a greater and more purposed prayer life, certainly makes it a worthwhile read. Prepare as you read it to be taken to a place with God of new heights, of fresh experiences, and of greater joy and success than you have ever known. I heartily recommend this book because I know the author—a great woman of prayer who learned these things in her own journey with the Father and His precious Son.

Dr. Ed King
Pastor, Redemption Church
Knoxville, Tennessee

# 30 days

## to a better prayer life

# nora king

30 DAYS TO A BETTER PRAYER LIFE
by Nora King

Parsons Publishing House
P. O. Box 488
Stafford, VA 22554 USA
www.ParsonsPublishingHouse.com
Info@ParsonsPublishingHouse.com

ISBN -13: 978-1-60273-012-0
ISBN -10: 1-60273-012-1
Library of Congress Control Number: 2010923699

Printed in the United States of America.
For World-Wide Distribution.

# DEDICATION

In memory of my precious son,

## MARCUS RAMSEY KING
### MAY 4, 1988 – MAY 21, 2005

*If it were not for the strength of
God imparted to me, I do not know
how I could make it through the
most difficult days of my entire life.*

# ACKNOWLEDGMENTS

Special recognition to my devoted
husband, Ed and my loving daughter,
Laren: *You are near and dear
to my heart. Your support and
encouragement are priceless. I
treasure you both.*

Thanks and appreciation to those who
helped me with the process of getting
this book to print: Wendy, Kathy, Laren,
Elizabeth, Hannah, Kate and Katy: *You
are great blessings!*

# FOREWORD

In the beginning, God desired someone with whom He could communicate and enjoy a special form of fellowship, so He created man. From the early chapters of Genesis it is very evident that Father God came daily to walk and talk with Adam and Eve. They enjoyed a time of close fellowship and communication.

In spite of Adam's failure, our heavenly Father did not give up on man. He is always available for some manner of communication. Prayer, regardless of the reason is a form of communing with God.

This book, *30 Days to A Better Prayer Life* is one of the best on this subject I have encountered in my more than sixty years of ministry. The book is direct, uncomplicated, instructive, and biblically sound. I am confident that as you put into practice the instructions in this book by Nora King you will discover your prayer life increasing, becoming more effective, and a vital everyday part of your life in Christ.

One's personal prayer life is extremely important and must be established or their spiritual life will remain undeveloped.

Noah Webster's dictionary has this to say about prayer, "Prayer, in a general sense, is the act of asking for a favor and particularly with earnestness."

I come from an era in which every Christian had a personal prayer life. If not, they, with the help of the Scripture and the Holy Spirit, were developing one. Prayers, for various reasons were never considered a light thing. Our churches often had all day prayer meetings and occasionally an all night prayer meeting with great results and attendance. Yet today, "prayer meetings" are almost a thing of the past and few Christians have a well developed prayer life.

My hat is off to Nora King, whom I have known for many years, for this inspiring book on this absolutely vital subject of a personal prayer life.

Nora and her husband, Ed, pastor the exciting congregation of Redemption Church in Knoxville, Tennessee. I am honored to have been asked to write the foreword for *30 Days to a Better Prayer Life*.

Hilton Sutton Th.D.
International Bible Teacher & Author

# INTRODUCTION

*"The earnest (heartfelt, continued) prayer of a righteous man makes tremendous power available [dynamic in its working]" (James 5:16, AMP).*

I have sensed God's pleasure and promptings as I have written on each individual day of prayer. I have discovered in my Christian walk the miraculous ability that can be released into my life and the lives of those for whom I am praying. You can enter your prayer closet and be used by God to make tremendous power available as described in the book of James. It isn't hit-or-miss or by chance that we receive answered prayer. We can obtain the biblical results promised in the Scripture if we learn how to pray more effectively. Prayer must be rooted in faith in God and in the belief of His Word. Then He will not only hear when we pray, but He has promised He will answer us. Through prayer—especially praying in the Spirit—I have gained greater insight into the supernatural realm, and I have grown sharper as a Pastor in hearing God speak to me about my life and ministry that affects others.

Prayer is also going into God's presence and allowing Him to renew and refresh us as we enjoy being with Him. Spiritual refreshing does come from being in His presence. Remember, prayer is not always asking or requesting. It can be simply talking things over with the Lord, quietly listening, or pouring out your heart to Him, while understanding He is there for you. Even in these times, we can be assured God will speak to us through His gentle voice, impress upon our hearts, or bring circumstances across our path to confirm His involvement in our lives.

As Christians, it is imperative that we familiarize ourselves with the Scriptures in order to know God's will. Prayer can never produce the results intended by the Lord unless we know and understand the Bible—our covenant with God. It's His legal document given to us. If we read it in the Scriptures, then it is the agreement God has made with us. When we pray we have the Word of God to give parameters and boundaries. In many cases, we can determine God's will for a specific situation simply by finding a promise in the Scriptures and then praying that particular truth. Christians who do not use the Bible as a guide in prayer can become misguided and unstable. There is no promise to grant our requests if we disregard His directions for prayer and do it our own way.

Prayer changes us and prayer changes what God is able to do in the world. He commissions us to bring His will upon the earth through prayer. One great saint of years gone by said, "It seems God will do nothing except a man should pray." I concur; intercessors have the power to change history because prayer is truly a lifeline or link to bring God's will from heaven to Earth. There is always hope as we talk to Him.

In over thirty years of pastoral ministry, I have taught many prayer principles, led copious prayer meetings, and encouraged many in their personal prayer life. My desire, through your reading this book, is to inspire and motivate you to engage in prayer as never before. By going through all of these prayer principles, I believe you will experience a notable difference. I trust you will gain strength through prayer day by day. As you read this book in the next 30 days, I pray that Jesus Christ will reveal Himself to you, open the door to hidden mysteries and divine secrets, impart wisdom, and that the Holy Spirit will touch your life with "fresh oil from heaven" (Psalm 92:10). May you be instructed and provoked to hunger for more fulfilling experiences in times of prayer with your Creator. May you gain marvelous insight into prayer, and may your partnership with the Heavenly Father be powerful, beneficial, and life-changing.

# TABLE OF CONTENTS

# DAY 1
# COURAGE

*"Also, {Jesus} told them a parable to the effect that they ought always to pray and not to turn coward (faint, lose heart, and give up)"* (Luke 18:1, AMP).

Jesus Himself encourages us to consistently pray and not give up or become hopeless in the circumstances of life. As believers, we need to be constant and steadfast in our prayer life. Consistency is not praying two hours one day then not praying for a week, and neither is it bringing something before the Lord in prayer one time, then dropping it. I will elaborate more on this later.

Consistency in prayer is a daily conversation with God; us conversing with Him and He talking to us. We need a designated prayer time; but, also understand that we can talk to Him in our car or as we go about our daily life. Including the Lord in whatever we do can change us: our attitude, our outlook, our responses, etc. There is nothing too insignificant for us to talk to the Lord about. He is interested in all aspects of our life.

After we petition the Lord in prayer initially, we do not have to continue to ask over and over again as if He did not hear us. Instead, make the petition or request and from that point on, we should pray by thanking Him that He heard us and that He is bringing our Scriptural prayers to pass. Philippians 4:6 says:

> *Do not fret or have any anxiety about anything, but in every circumstance and in everything by prayer and petition [definite requests] with thanksgiving continue to make your wants known to God (AMP).*

You can see from this Scripture that we are told not to be anxious or worry about anything, but to trust God in everything we face and talk to Him in prayer in definite ways. State what we need, and then thank Him as we continue to bring it up to Him in the future. Praying in this way, we will not erode or destroy our faith! Mark 11:24 says to believe we receive when we pray. We can ask the Lord to reveal anything associated with our prayer request that He would have us pray about more thoroughly—details, etc. He has the ability to bring revelation, enlightenment, and insight to us as we pray. In doing this, we may even grasp a better understanding of what is needed to bring our request to pass or possibly what hindrances stand in the way. Through prayer, we can actually bind up and stand against hindrances and allow the power of the Holy Spirit to move them as we partner with God.

As the trials of life and weariness come to assail us, we will not faint when we remain constant in our prayer life. It is easy to lose heart, become discouraged, and give up, but God has put strength on the inside of His Spirit-filled believers. Even in the midst of wanting to give up mentally or emotionally, God has given us the capability, through our prayer connection with Him, to persevere in spite of opposition. It seems that continued prayer and fellowship with God keeps us stirred in our spirits and forbids the devil from being successful in discouraging and robbing us.

As we stay connected to Him through our praying, we allow God's strength to work in us and be dominant in our lives. It will propel us when we feel we cannot go on or when we do not want to go on. It is safe to say that every one of us have had times when we wanted to quit or give up. If we stay in communication and fellowship with God through prayer, we will have strength to persevere and overcome. Continuing in prayer is the key to receiving His power in order not to faint, lose heart, or give up. Through our fellowship connection with the Lord endurance in a greater measure is made available.

# PRAYER

*Lord, help me to be consistent in my prayer life. May I not give up or lose heart in what I am seeking. I desire to persevere and to be strong in the Holy Spirit in the midst of difficulty.*

*Thank you for an impartation of renewed strength in prayer.*

# DAY 2
# DYNAMIC PRAYER

*"The earnest (heartfelt, continued) prayer of a right-
eous man makes tremendous power available [dy-
namic in its working]"* (James 5:16, AMP).

Elijah was human just like you and me. He
was neither perfect nor always spiritual; but
when he prayed, he prayed effectively, fervently,
and sincerely. God is revealing to us that while
we, too, may be imperfect, we can still receive
answers to our prayers in time of need. The
Living Bible says it this way, "The earnest prayer
of a righteous man has great power and wonderful results." When you pray sincere, honest,
and heartfelt prayers, it will release miracle-
working power that will produce a marvelous outcome.

The Amplified Bible says that effective, fervent prayer "makes tremendous power available
[dynamic in its working]." Your words spoken to

God go to work to tear down obstacles when this tremendous power is released through prayer. The contrary is also true. When we do not pray, we do not avail ourselves of the miraculous insight that God has made accessible to us; we continue to suffer and struggle through the circumstances of life. Powerful spiritual energy can be released through prayer to combat the works of darkness and help us receive our miracle breakthrough.

One cold and snowy day, a group of us were gathered together on a staff retreat to spend a few days in the beautiful Smoky Mountains. When we arrived, we discovered that we had no water due to frozen water pipes. I, for one, did not want to spend time without water with a group where there would be no way to cook, bathe, etc. So, I asked everyone to agree with me in prayer according to Matthew 18:19 that the water would flow through those pipes. You see, it's not up to me to figure out how this could happen or to reason out an answer in my mind, I am simply to believe and ask! We prayed a prayer and before the prayer was over, water began to rush out of the faucets! This may seem trivial to some, but not to me when I would have to be in a very uncomfortable setting for a few days. This prayer request was not insignificant to God either. He is concerned about every aspect of our lives. We should not be ambivalent in prayer, but steadfast believing nothing is impossible to God because He cares about and is interested in our lives! There is power to change things—prayer power!

If there is tremendous, immense power and might released into our world when we pray over a need or desire to change our circumstances, then why are many Christians not sincerely praying? It could be that we are lacking knowledge and understanding or we are apathetic in our spiritual life. If we are in one of these two categories, the good news is that we can change and take the Lord at His Word. Then, we will see dynamic happenings in our lives through prayer.

As you can see, God will do outstanding things for us when we pray. God tells us to "ask and you will receive." He then says in another Scripture, "You have not because you ask not or because you have wrong motives" (James 4:2-3). We need to be conscious of our responsibility to ask God for answers and check our motives and make sure they are right. Then, we can pray and take advantage of the tremendous power available through prayer! This power will change our world.

# PRAYER

*Lord, thank You for the miracle-working power of the Holy Spirit that is made available to me through fervent, heartfelt prayer. May my motives be correct and pure. Help me not to neglect the privilege of prayer.*

# DAY 3
# "DARE TO" PRAYER

*"Now unto him that is able to do exceeding abun-
dantly above all that we ask or think, according to
the power that worketh in us"* (Ephesians 3:20).

*"If ye abide in me, and my words abide in you,
ye shall ask what ye will, and it shall be done
unto you"* (John 15:7).

God is able to go far beyond whatever we
ask or even dream of in prayer. This is possible
through the resurrection power of God that's at
work in us. Resurrection power raised Jesus
Christ from the dead and is available to the believer if we know, understand, and believe it.
God is able to do extraordinary things for us and
through us because this same power that raised
Jesus from the dead is working in us. Nothing is
impossible with God. Nothing is too difficult for
Him. He is the One that parted the Red Sea,
closed the lion's mouth for Daniel, protected men

in the fiery furnace, and enabled a youthful David to take down and behead a giant! Do you have "giant" problems or circumstances that loom before you? Take heart. Let us, without fear, dare to pray and ask God. Allow His empowerment present in us to come to our aid in times of difficulty and behead life's great problems.

We need to be bold in prayer! Hebrews 4:16 tells us to come before God's throne of grace boldly and find mercy when we need help. Come fearlessly, not timidly and cowering. We are told that, as Christians, we can do this when we confess our sin to the Lord and forsake it; we are forgiven and cleansed by the blood of Jesus. We do not have to accept the guilt and condemnation that the devil would try to heap upon us or that our own mind would try to cling to. We are again made acceptable to ask boldly for our needs to be met. It states in the Amplified Bible that we are to be courageous and "dare" to ask and it shall be done.

John 15:7 gives us great insight into prayer. It tells us if we continue to live our lives abiding in the heavenly Father through Jesus Christ, whatever we ask will be done. To *abide* in Christ means our relationship is not a casual one, but is a relationship where we are committed to pleasing and obeying the Lord in all our ways as best we can. We, of course, understand we are not perfect or trying to receive from Him through our own works, but because of our love for God and dedication to Him, we must strive to please and be obedient. His desires actually become ours because of our unity and oneness with the Lord. It is in this condition that we can ask what we desire and it shall—not maybe, but **shall** be done.

From these Scriptures, we realize the miraculous power of the Holy Spirit is mightily working in us so we can boldly dare to ask God for our needs and desires to be met. There is no shortage of power to bring it to pass. We should not accept the guilt, condemnation, or lies that Satan brings against us, but cast away his scheme and deceit. Resist him in Jesus' Name. Then, we can have confidence in prayer because we are living our lives anchored in and abiding in Jesus Christ.

# PRAYER

*Father, in Jesus' Name, help me to be courageous in prayer and experience Your power at work in me. May I continually be settled in You. Knowing that I can ask what I desire, and it most assuredly shall be done.*

# DAY 4
# AGREEMENT

*"Again I say unto you, that if two of you shall agree on earth as touching any thing that they shall ask, it shall be done for them of my Father which is in heaven"* (Matthew 18:19).

Jesus gave a wonderful promise that is available to all Christians when we pray in agreement with other believers. In this Scripture, Jesus repeats the emphatic word, "shall." He said **shall** agree; **shall** ask; and it **shall** be done. We know that God does not lie; therefore, if He says to agree and to ask, then the Father, which is in heaven, shall do it for us. This is a prayer principle that is simple, but profound and much overlooked.

Not only does Jesus tell us that it shall be done for us, but He also does not put restrictions on what we can ask of Him. James tells us that we **do not have** because we **do not ask**! Often, we go through turbulent times for a while before it dawns on us to talk to the Father and ask for His help.

Obviously, we should be asking for things that He has promised us in the Scriptures which are godly and lawful. He cannot and will not grant to us things that are ungodly, sinful, or contrary to the Word of God. This is one reason that we need to know the principles found in the Bible. God's Word is His will for us. When we see, hear, and understand that a promise is ours, then we will not be asking the Lord for things contrary to His will. He is no respecter of persons, and He is waiting for His children to dare to believe His Word. Once we see and hear it for ourselves, faith can arise for us to receive what belongs to us.

This verse from the Amplified Bible gives us a broader understanding of Jesus' words:

> If two of you on Earth agree (harmonize together, make a symphony together) about whatever [anything and everything] they may ask, it will come to pass and be done for them by My Father in heaven (Matthew 18:19, AMP).

The heavenly Father desires and expects believers to unify and release the powerful force of faith in prayer to move mountains, if necessary.

A magnificent sound is that of symphonic instruments playing together in the same key and bringing harmony to our ears. This harmony in prayer is what God desires for us. We must come together centered on our prayer request. That's beautiful music to God's ears! This does not mean that two people must be of the same denominational persuasion and have the exact same beliefs on every point; it simply means that the two believers must be operating with the same faith in believing God for the answer to their prayer request. Unity among the saints is amazing and supernaturally powerful.

Agreement and harmony will not be achieved if one person is operating in doubt, fear, or unbelief while the other actively releases their faith. Praying together, especially as a married couple, is priceless because harmonizing in prayer can produce remarkable results in our families and homes. If you are not married, find another Christian who believes this prayer principle and pray with them.

In order to be in one accord, believers must be living their lives in God's love and forgiveness towards others. Unforgiveness, unkindness, etc., will stop the promises of God from coming to us and prohibit our needed answers from manifesting. Therefore, we cannot afford to hold grudges and mistreat others. Drop it and let it go. God is love; so if He is in us, He will prompt us to love others even when they are unlovely and forgive them for a suffered or a perceived wrong.

# PRAYER

*Lord, thank You for the power of prayer agreement. Help me to be in harmony with Your Word and with Your Spirit concerning my life. Give me other Christians who will pray with me concerning the needs and desires of my life. I, in turn, will commit to pray with others for theirs.*

# DAY 5
# ABIDING

*If ye abide in me, and my words abide in you, ye shall*
*ask what ye will, and it shall be done unto you"*
(John 15:7).

The Bible consists of the Old Testament and the New Testament. It is a testament or a covenant between God and man. A *covenant* is essentially a binding agreement or a contract. In any contract, the acts and responsibilities of those entering into it are specified. The contract also defines the results or the consequences, should one of the parties default or breech it.

The Bible is God's covenant with a person who enters into a relationship with Him. The Word of God is filled with many promises. These promises are conditional to our remaining in fellowship with, or abiding in, God. Just as a loved one who has passed away and has left behind a will stating their desires for those remaining, their will is faithfully carried out. So it is with God's will—the Scriptures. He has provided greatly for us. If we meet the criteria or requirements, He will stand behind it to enforce it.

According to **Webster's Dictionary**, "abide" means *to wait for; to endure without yielding; to remain stable or fixed in a state; to continue in a place.* It also means *to live or dwell; make our home.* We can see from these definitions that abiding signifies permanence. *Abiding* is not being continually in and out of fellowship with God. *Abiding* conveys the meaning of settling down and dwelling.

Jesus says that if we will uphold our end of the contract by abiding in the Word, God Himself will uphold His end of the contract by answering our prayers. Hopefully, it goes without saying our requests and petitions have to be within the parameters of God's Word. We cannot expect to be granted things that are sinful or contrary to God's Word. That is why it is so important to be familiar with the Scriptures and regularly read the Bible.

For many years I struggled with knowing God's will. He is not like humans—up and down emotionally. He's not schizophrenic saying, "yes," then "no"! He is steadfast, dependable, and reliable. We can count on Him to do what He has said. On Earth, we can disappoint each other or let someone down, but He is faithful in every situation. We can begin to discover His will by reading the Bible.

Our covenant with God is filled with all the precious promises to meet our every need. When we abide in Him and allow His words to abide in us, then we will be able to make genuine requests. Then we can confidently, reverently, and humbly expect and believe that God will answer our prayers.

# PRAYER

*Lord, help me to be steadfast and stable; always abiding in You. May I understand Your will and the good plan You have for my life. I want my heart to be Your heart. As I make my requests and petitions to You, I have an assurance they will be done.*

# DAY 6
# MAKE A DIFFERENCE

*"And I sought for a man among them that should make up the hedge, and stand in the gap before me for the land, that I should not destroy it: but I found none"* (Ezekiel 22:30).

God is actively seeking and searching for someone to fill the gap by praying for people and nations. A person who stands in that gap is called an *intercessor.* This means we take the hand of God on one side and the hand of the person in need on the other and bring them together through prayer. God needs intercessors to pray in order for His will to be done in the earth. God is seeking; God is looking. God is searching for people to place a hedge of protection around a person or nation, and it happens through prayer.

E. M. Bounds said, "The prayers of God's saints are the capital stock in heaven by which Christ carries on His great work upon the earth."

It is through the prayers of believers like you and me that God chooses to step into the affairs of mankind.

It's been said that history belongs to the intercessor. As intercessors, we have the power to change the events on the earth by receiving divine intervention from heaven. God desires to assist in the affairs of men and is waiting on us to call on Him to ask for His help.

Intercessors are enforcers of God's will upon the earth. If we think that the devil is going to allow the will of God to be done without an intercessor as an enforcer, we are sorely misinformed. How often have we watched and allowed the enemy to come in and wreak havoc in our lives, our local church, or our nation without calling out to God? We must not be paralyzed by apathy or passivity, but stir ourselves to seek God in prayer. Sometimes we are willing to pray and intercede; other times, we are listless and act as though "there's no use." God said that He looked for a man to make up the hedge, but He found none. Let's not allow that to be said of us. You're the man!

It's possible to become an enforcer of God's will. We can readily understand His will for mankind through His Holy Word. We then make that promise our prayer—this is being an enforcer. We can pray and make a definite difference on behalf of people, our nation, and our spiritual and governmental leadership (2 Timothy 2:1-40).

Each of us has a sphere of influence that God has given to us, just as He gave Jesus the twelve disciples. Jesus prayed for them and they rocked the world with the Gospel (John 17:24). We can't be responsible for praying for everyone, but we can pray for those we are involved with and the needs that come to our attention. Then, God can "rock" the world through our lives.

If WE do not intercede and pray, perhaps no one will...

# PRAYER

*Lord, help me to think soberly concerning intercession. I acknowledge that You have given me a realm of influence concerning my family, my work place, my church family, my nation, and the world. I purpose to be sensitive to Your promptings to pray for others today.*

# DAY 7
# COMMITMENT

*"And he went a little farther, and fell on his face, and prayed, saying, O my Father, if it be possible, let this cup pass from me: nevertheless not as I will, but as thou wilt"* (Matthew 26:39).

We know that Jesus was a man of prayer. There are many examples throughout the New Testament where Jesus pulled away from the crowd and the hustle and bustle of life to pray. He also prayed with His disciples and prayed with the multitudes. He truly modeled for us a life of prayer. Jesus had a close relationship with the Father that was possible through intimacy that came from His times of prayer. Through spending time with the Lord, we can acquire His heart, His attitude, and His nature to become more Christ-like.

We see Jesus in the Garden of Gethsemane understanding what He was going to have to face and dealing with the great struggles attached to that awareness. He asked the Father if there was another way other than His crucifixion and death for the redemption of mankind to be completed. Jesus was cognizant of the plan of redemption because it had been laid out before the foundation of the world, and He knew the great price that would have to be paid. He still humbly prayed and finished with, "Not My will, but Your will be done," submitting Himself wholly to the Father. I cannot begin to fathom nor imagine the deep painful emotions He had to face that day alone in the garden. The Bible tells us Jesus was in such anguish of soul, He began to sweat great drops of blood.

Far too often, people interpret this Scripture as the way to pray in all situations: "If it be Your will, Lord." Certainly, there are times we need to pray to determine the will of God - submitting to the plan of God for our lives. However, this is only one type of prayer taught in the New Testament. So, we do not have to end every prayer with "if it be your will!"

In many cases, the Bible itself tells us the will of God. We have the ability to read the Word of God and know what His will is in various circumstances. We, by faith, accept what He has said and receive it as done. When it comes to salvation, healing, protection, or provision, we do not have to pray, "If it be Your will." We already know His will and understand what He has rescued us from: the curse of sickness, poverty, and hell. It is revealed to us through Galatians 3:13-14 that Jesus redeemed us from the curse and gave us the promise of the Spirit. Therefore, we do not end our prayer for these things with, "If it be Your will." To reiterate, we only pray, "If it be Your wien we are committing or consecrating ourselves to the Lord for His purpose for our lives, just as Jesus did. We surrender ourselves to His design.

The lesson in this Scripture to me is that Jesus lived a prayer-filled life. We know at this particular time He prayed at least one hour as He awakened the disciples and asked them, "What! Could you not watch with Me one hour?" (Matthew 26:40). Isn't that just like us today? Many times we mean well, but like the men who surrounded Jesus, we are tired, hurried, or just don't seem to be able to finish our prayer assignments for one reason or another. I am so thankful that God doesn't give up on us. Aren't you?

Also, we can see that Jesus did not pray from a selfish perspective. He prayed, "Not My will but Your will be done." The objective of this kind of prayer in our own lives should not be to convince God to do something for us. The objective of this honest prayer is to get ourselves aligned with the will of God. Not my will, but Your will be done, Lord. This is a true prayer of submission and commitment.

Ephesians 6:18 reads, "Praying always with all prayer and supplication in the Spirit, and watching thereunto with all perseverance and supplication for all saints." One translation says pray "with all manner" of prayer. Another translation says "different kinds" of prayer. Again, praying, "Lord, if it be Your will," is only one kind of prayer; there are various kinds of prayer with specific guidelines for us to use when we approach the heavenly Father. We will continue to explain the different kinds of prayer more specifically as the days progress.

# PRAYER

*Lord, help me to develop a more intimate prayer life. May my will be aligned with Your will. I pray I will become or remain dedicated, submissive, and consecrated to You.*

# DAY 8
# VIOLENT PRAYER

*And from the days of John the Baptist until the present time, the kingdom of heaven has endured violent assault, and violent men seize it by force [as a precious prize—a share in the heavenly kingdom is sought with most ardent zeal and intense exertion]* (Matthew 11:12, AMP).

*"From the days of John the Baptist until now the kingdom of heaven has been forcefully advancing and forceful men lay hold of it"* (Matthew 11:12, NIV).

People living for the Lord and doing the work of God have endured violent attacks over the years. The Bible is saying that the devil and the world system may try to overthrow a Christian, but "violent" men clutch to what God has promised in Scripture to achieve their desired result and advance the Kingdom of God. Consider what the great Bible teacher Gordon

Lindsay once said regarding prayer: "A Christian should pray one violent prayer every day." I concur with that! We need to not give up too easily on God's promises when we're under attack, but determine when we pray that the devil cannot withhold. The Lord is pleased when we emphatically pray the Scriptures to Him; it releases power to counteract against the kingdom of darkness. This is a violent prayer.

We should have zeal and intensity in our praying as this text indicates. Jesus defeated and conquered the enemy; through His death on the cross and His resurrection, He reduced Satan's actual power over us to zero as Colossians reveals. Therefore, we should be aware that we are the heavenly Father's enforcer of promises given through Scripture. Satan may try to resist, but he cannot withstand the power of God's Word spoken in faith by a believer. Thus, we are forcefully advancing and laying hold of what belongs to us.

A violent prayer is not one in which we have to scream, yell, or raise our voice; it is when we see a promise in the Word of God and receive it by faith and deny every spirit of darkness the right to withhold it from us. A violent prayer superimposes the truth of Scripture over a situation. Passivity stands by and gives up, but the violent or tenacious prayer refuses to let His promises go. I am not indicating we are to be in anyway disrespectful or arrogant to the Lord, but confidently bring our covenant agreement to Him, while at the same time forbidding the devil the right to lie to us or steal from us.

As Christians, we can be militant in the spirit and have zeal in our praying while at the same time being gentle, kind, and sweet in our demeanor when we deal with others. We can and should seize what God has given to us. We need to be aggressive in prayer concerning things from which we have already been redeemed, standing fiercely against: poverty, sickness, defeat, and lack (Galatians 3:13-14). God doesn't get upset with us; we treat Him with reverence, but show no mercy on the devil.

We must make a demand on the Scripture; make a demand on the power and rights that have been given to us by God. Just as we make a demand on electricity which is present and available, but is not enabled until the switch is turned on. In the same way, we are enabled by God in our prayer life. The "switch" is faith in God and His Word without doubting. God has made His supernatural power available to us through prayer. Pray, believe God, and experience the power of God being "switched" on and working in your life.

# PRAYER

*Lord, I desire to be zealous and violent—determined in prayer. Help me to be militant in the Spirit against those things Jesus redeemed me from. By the power of Your Holy Spirit, I will make a demand on Your promises that I see in the Scriptures, and I will not relent. I want to be one of Your forceful believers who advance the Kingdom through my prayer life. Give me passion for the things that You are passionate about.*

# DAY 9
# FORGIVENESS

*"And when ye stand praying, forgive, if ye have ought against any: that your Father also which is in heaven may forgive you your trespasses"* (Mark 11:25).

In this verse, Jesus presents to us an extraordinary prayer principle for receiving answers to our prayers: forgiveness. We, as believers, are commanded to love others; in fact, the walk of love is the foundation of our faith. Our faith works or operates by continually abiding in love toward the Lord and other people. In Galatians 5:6 it says, "...faith which worketh by love," or faith that is powered by love. Because of this, we must release individuals who have hurt or wounded us by actively forgiving them and allowing the person and the circumstances to be loosed from us.

In Mark 11:25, Jesus is teaching us another foundational truth regarding prayer. He is saying we can have an open line of communication with the Father, or it can be stopped and short-circuited by not forgiving others. If we want God to hear and answer our prayers, we must be mindful of our relationships with others. Whether family, friends, church members, or co-workers, we must remember that if we are holding grudges or if we are not forgiving toward others, God will not hear us when we talk to Him. We may pray and ask God for the things we need, but God says that if we are in unforgiveness, He cannot hear and answer our petitions. As Christians, we must recognize and put a stop to the camouflaged trap of unforgiveness.

Jesus is clearly speaking and attempting to get a message to believers. That message is this: "Forgive, let it go, give it to Me, and don't hold on." If you clutch unforgiveness, you can grow bitter, harsh, and unkind.

A woman in the book of Ruth called Naomi had grown bitter towards God because she suffered a great loss when her husband and sons had died, and she was left alone. Bitterness and unforgiveness towards God imprisoned her to the point that even her appearance and countenance changed. People who knew her from the past didn't recognize her when she returned to her hometown. She even said: "'Don't call me *Naomi (pleasant)*,' she told them. 'Call me *Mara (bitter)*, because the Almighty has made my life very bitter'" (Ruth 1:20, NIV).

34

Once unforgiveness sets in, bitterness will totally change us from one controlled by the gentleness of the Holy Spirit to one marked by harshness and hardness. I have faced great tragedy to the point of despair of life and was tempted to turn inward, lash out, and blame God and anyone else for my pain and suffering. Instead, I chose to release it to the Lord and trust Him when I didn't understand, and fall at the foot of His cross until the Holy Spirit could do His restorative work in me. In myself, I could have been like Naomi, but thankfully I chose God's method.

By the way, Naomi eventually experienced God's favor in her life; she did not remain bitter. Is it easy to drop things and let them go when we have been hurt or wounded by someone? Absolutely not. Although forgiving someone can be one of the most difficult things we have to do, it is imperative that we release suffered or perceived wrongs if we want God to hear and answer our prayers. In our time of need, Jesus taught us in Matthew chapter six that if we forgive others of their trespasses against us, our heavenly Father will forgive us. If we do not forgive others of their offenses against us, neither will the Father forgive us. We all need forgiveness and we all need answered prayers. If we are wise, we will forgive; unforgiveness costs us too much.

# PRAYER

*Lord, thank You for the power of forgiveness. Help me to forgive everyone, and sometimes it may even be You. I am able to live a forgiving lifestyle because You first forgave me. Cause me to be released from hurts, wounds, and bitterness as I forgive others and let go of perceived or intentional wrongs done to me. Through this cleansing process, I know the way is opened for You to hear and answer my prayers.*

# DAY 10
# HIS GOODNESS

*"I had fainted, unless I had believed to see the good-ness of the Lord in the land of the living. Wait on the Lord: be of good courage, and he shall strengthen thine heart. Wait, I say, on the Lord"* (Psalm 27:13-14).

The Psalmist David is giving us the key to victorious living: waiting upon the Lord. Spending time in communion with the Creator of the universe through praise and adoration is a part of waiting upon the Lord. Making this a portion of our daily time with God will glorify Him and sensitize our own hearts to His presence, and it will silence the devil (Psalm 8:2, NIV). Praise and worship is a form of prayer.

David said that he would have fainted, or lost his strength to persevere in times of trouble and difficulty, had he not believed to see and experience the goodness of God. We must believe God is a good God and gives benefits and blessings to His people. Believing in a good God who will protect, deliver, bless, and prosper His family implies we have hope. Without hope we will not maintain strength to endure in turbulent times, but we will lose heart and become discouraged. David, who is said to be a man after God's own heart, knew that God was good. In this Psalm, David tells us that as we wait, worship, and serve the Lord, we don't have to live disheartened and weakened because He will bring His strength to us and enable us. We are in His presence, not petitioning Him, but magnifying and lifting Him up above anything and everything. Magnifying enlarges an object and causes other things around it to almost disappear. Worshipping the Lord will make God greater and more powerful in our lives.

How many times have we heard "spiritual" people say that God's blessings to us will only be realized in heaven? Some will make fun of those who believe that God will bless us here on the earth—not just when we get to heaven. Yes, we certainly lay up treasures in heaven and blessings will abound there, but God also wants to bless our lives here and now. He wants to impart to us abundant life (John 10:10). Just as an earthly father desires to bless and favor his own children, so the heavenly Father desires that for His own family. We all face problems, but God has pledged He will deliver us out of them all if we follow His directions.

As we wait on the Lord through praise, worship, and thanksgiving, He will sometimes speak to us. The Lord can give us direction in our lives even when we aren't expecting it. He can provide a word that will encourage us, strengthen us, and sometimes correct our course. God desires to talk to us to help us avoid pitfalls in our lives, just as we want to give direction and guidance to our own children. When He is speaking—are we listening?

David was emphatic when he said, "wait on the Lord...wait, I say, on the Lord." As we are engaged in this manner of prayer by worshipping and waiting patiently before Him, He will be glorified. Through His presence in our lives, we will be spiritually charged and strengthened. Worship Him with all your heart—that is genuine prayer.

# PRAYER

*Lord, I thank You that You are a good God. I will wait on You. As I serve and minister to You through praise, worship, and thanksgiving, be glorified. Shape and mold my life as I am in Your presence.*

# DAY 11
# GUARDING

*"I have set watchmen upon thy walls,
O Jerusalem, which shall never hold their
peace day nor night: ye that make mention of the
lord, keep not silence"* (Isaiah 62:6).

During biblical times, cities were surrounded by walls for protection. The watchmen
were stationed upon the walls to stand guard and
keep watch for predators and enemies. When the
watchmen saw an enemy approaching, they
would cry out to alert the citizens. Then the
people could prepare to effectively defend themselves and their city.

The same is true for the church; intercessors can be watchmen (people who pray).
Through intercessory prayer, we are to stand as a
guard and pray concerning needs that are revealed to us. In our place of prayer, we can receive a knowing or a revelation. God wants us to

speak out and mention the God-given insight which He gives as we are praying. In this way, the Holy Spirit can prepare the way for our victory when we cooperate with Him.

We are to be alert in prayer; we must intercede and ask God for His divine intervention. God needs a man on the earth to ask or pray before He intervenes in the affairs of men (Ezekiel 22:30). One great godly man of old said, "It seems God will do nothing on the earth except a man will pray." Prayer needs to be perpetual, ongoing, and continuous. We are to pray without ceasing (1 Thessalonians 5:17) and not give up. This doesn't mean we pray twenty-four/seven, but it is a lifestyle where we seize every opportunity to make a prayer difference. I pray in the car, at the supermarket or wherever. People may not know I'm talking to the Lord, but I am. If I see someone on the side of the road in a car accident, or someone distraught, etc., I just breathe out a prayer to the Father and ask Him to intervene on their behalf and help them. I call this my "breath prayers." I may never see this person again or know of their condition, but I do know the Holy Spirit is present to assist and bring comfort and peace. In this way, I am a watchman.

We are told to not be quiet or silent when we see injustice or evil, wrongdoing, or demonic activity. Our responsibility is to cry out to God and not be passive or speechless. We are to continually speak His Word: mentioning the promises we find, reminding God of what He has said in his Word, and reminding the devil of what God has said. In Isaiah 55:11, we are told His spoken Word will accomplish what it is sent forth to do. We are not to be silent or quiet; do not shut your mouth. Do not stop speaking the Word of God as you pray. The Scriptures are powerful and they can blast mountainous problems out of the way to attain triumph.

Continue to be the one who comes before the Lord on behalf of someone else in need. Do not give up on the things God has placed in your spirit to pray. These areas need your prayer efforts: your friends, your family, your church, the nation, the world, and the great harvest of souls.

Keep alert and remain engaged in prayer as a partner with God Himself. Be a vigilant watchman.

# PRAYER

*Lord, thank You for the power and privilege of intercessory prayer. Thank You that I can stand as a watchman concerning my family's life and the life of my church family and those You bring to my attention. I will not be quiet, but will continue to pray Your life-changing words over people and situations.*

# DAY 12
# MIND GAMES

*"O God the Lord, the strength of my
salvation, thou hast covered my head in
the day of battle"* (Psalm 140:7).

In ancient days, a village would often be on a hillside. When attacks would come on a city, the men approaching would hold a shield over their heads to protect them from the debris being hurled at them. Comparatively, we are the ones going up the hillside to take or receive what belongs to us. The devil may be throwing evil, faith-robbing, fearful thoughts to our left, right and all around. However, remember that in the very hour of his vicious attack, you have been given the proper armor to control your thoughts to win the battle. Think upon His promises, His provision, His love, and remember this keeps your head or mind protected and covered.

Jesus Christ, through His death, burial, and resurrection, became our deliverer and our rescuer from both sin and Satan's deceptive power. When we are in a battle, circumstances can be difficult to bare, and we can be hindered and unable to pray effectively. We must enter into our prayer closet to talk with the Lord about our challenges as we find ourselves blasted with thoughts of fear, failure, and inadequacy. The battlefield in which Satan uses his power to try to overthrow us takes place in our mind. That is what this particular Scripture is saying. The thoughts and fears hurled at us are intended to discourage us and cause us to give up and quit. But, this Scripture tells us that when we are in the middle of warfare, God has given us the ability to lay hold of protection from the mental onslaughts the devil brings our way. Through our communion with God via the Scriptures and in prayer, we are empowered to defeat these mind-game attacks and receive our salvation (deliverance) from God Almighty.

We are to react and deal with the thoughts of fear and failure that the evil forces of darkness bring to snare us. Ignoring the thoughts will not make them go away. Satan is a liar and deceiver. We must not be deluded into accepting what he says as truth. Always answer the devil when he speaks his lies by telling him the truth of God's Word. Matthew 6:31 says, "Take no thought saying..." When we speak out of our own mouth the things Satan is whispering to us, we are "buying" into and cooperating with his deceptive plan. We must not give or lend our voices to it. Second Corinthians 10:5 tells us to throw off these thoughts like we would a dirty, soiled garment. We must not receive them; instead, receive the Lord's deliverance. Then we must counteract evil thoughts with faith-filled truths in agreement with the Scriptures and begin to SPEAK them out.

Philippians 4:8 says:

*Finally, brethren, whatsoever things are true, whatsoever things are honest, whatsoever things are just, whatsoever things are pure, whatsoever things are lovely, whatsoever things are of good report; if there be any virtue, and if there be any praise, think on these things.*

This instructs us to think upon truthful things. The book of John says, "Thy Word is truth." The Bible is ultimate truth. Thus, when we approach God our minds can be focused and assured that even in the heat of battle, He's got us covered from the onslaught of vicious mental attacks.

# PRAYER

*Lord, teach me to keep my mind on You and Your Word in troubled times and not to fall into the enemy's trap by allowing him to defeat me through deceitful mental attacks. May I be quick to answer back the lies that are contrary to Your truth.*

# DAY 13
# REFRESHING

*Ask ye of the Lord rain in the time of the latter rain; so the lord shall make bright clouds, and give them showers of rain, to every one grass in the field* (Zechariah 10:1).

In this passage, we are told that in the time God is pouring out His Holy Spirit in the earth, we are to ask Him to touch our lives so that we would be refreshed and revived spiritually. Isaiah 60:1-2 says:

*Arise, shine; for thy light is come, and the glory of the Lord is risen upon thee. For, behold, the darkness shall cover the earth, and gross darkness the people: but the Lord shall arise upon thee, and His glory shall be seen upon thee.*

These words communicate to us to rise up from spiritual inactivity and allow our light to shine in this dark world. We are to be awakened out of spiritual sluggishness to receive zeal and renewed enthusiasm so that we overflow with God's presence.

Also, in this Scripture, we are told that great darkness or evil would be over the earth and overpowering darkness would be upon the people. This means there will be severe mental depression on mankind in the last days. I believe we are in those times now. Many are depressed, troubled, and being oppressed—living life with an ominous cloud over their lives, feeling that there is no way out. The antidote for this heavy cloud of depression is to allow the light of God's Word to radiate and dispel this blanket of darkness. The hopeless can receive a sense of expectancy and see a glimmer of light as God's people rise up and allow the Holy Spirit to shine through their lives.

Hungering and thirsting for the Lord and the things of God are vital to combat the darkness in these last days. We read in the Bible that many will grow cold in their relationship with Him and become entangled and weighed down in the affairs of this life. Luke 21:34-36 says:

> *And take heed to yourselves, lest at any time your hearts be overcharged (overloaded) with surfeiting (over indul-*

*gence), and drunkenness, and cares of this life, and so that day come upon you unawares. For as a snare shall it come on all them that dwell on the face of the whole earth. Watch ye therefore, and pray always, that ye may be accounted worthy to escape all these things that shall come to pass, and to stand before the Son of man.*

We are to live on guard so as not to allow life to overwhelm us by being fully absorbed with our own schedule, agenda, or life's worries and anxieties. These things are intended by the devil to be a hidden trap that can surely ensnare. We actually guard or defend ourselves through prayer.

The Word of God also tells us that if we hunger and thirst, we would be filled (Matthew 5:6). Therefore strongly desiring the things of God, thirsting for the Holy Spirit, and praying for His rain is not only good, it is life-changing. We will be enabled to stay aglow or on fire for the Lord and not be emptied, unsatisfied, and entangled in life's cares.

Psalm 92:10 says, "I shall be anointed with fresh oil." Oil is symbolic of the Holy Spirit. No matter how many times we have been touched by the Holy Spirit, a fresh outpouring is always to be desired. We can become spiritually stale, cold, and indifferent if we go about life without following the instructions of Scripture on how to stay full of the Holy Spirit. We cannot rely on what has happened in the past, but we need a fresh impartation of His presence in our lives NOW. Ephesians 5:18-20 also gives us insight on remaining revived and renewed by singing to the Lord and praising Him.

The rain is also symbolic of the Holy Spirit which we need to cleanse and restore us. Through our times of praying, the refreshing rain of the Holy Spirit is available to us for the asking.

# PRAYER

*Lord, touch my life with the outpouring of Your Spirit in these last days. Help me not to grow cold, apathetic, and complacent. Cause hunger, thirst, and the fire of God to always be present in my life.*

# DAY 14
# WEAPONRY

*"For the weapons of our warfare are not carnal,
but mighty through God to the pulling down
of strong holds"* (2 Corinthians 10:4).

God has given us everything we need for the spiritual battles we face in life. It is wonderful to know that we have not been left to our own devices and reasoning while under attack. Because of Almighty God, we have complete access to spiritual weaponry, tools, and armor (Ephesians 6:11-17); we have everything required to win the war to displace the devil's forceful barrage. The Message Bible says it this way:

> *We use our powerful God-tools for
> smashing warped philosophies, tearing
> down barriers erected against the truth
> of God, fitting every loose thought and
> emotion and impulse into the structure
> of life shaped by Christ. Our tools are
> ready at hand for clearing the ground of*

*every obstruction and building lives of obedience into maturity* (2 Corinthians 10:3, MSG).

From this translation, you can readily understand Paul is referring to the battleground of the mind. This is where we wrestle our thoughts, capture them, and bring them into obedience to the Scriptures.

As a part of the body of Christ, we have been equipped with an arsenal to handle whatever is thrown our way. Getting our thoughts, emotions, and impulses under spiritual control is essential to victory. We cannot allow fear of failure and inability to cloud and push the Word of God out of our hearts and minds. We cannot use the world's weapons and means of battle to try to change situations; we must use the spiritual weapons which God has given us in order to see real change.

Let's look at a few of our God-given weapons: love defeats hate; faith destroys fear and unbelief; prayer deflates hopelessness, discouragement, and passivity; forgiveness releases us by breaking the chains of hurt, offense, resentment, and bitterness; worship and praise allows the manifested presence of God to come on the scene and quiet the devil. To the evil, unseen world, these instruments are potent, destructive, and giant-killing.

The world is overflowing with mass confusion and deception concerning the real truth. The times in which we live are filled with many voices that are contending for our attention and trying to intervene in our affairs. However, God has given believers a clear voice through the Scriptures and the Holy Spirit which penetrates deceit and hidden agendas. This clear voice can come to us in our prayer closet. This communication from the Lord in prayer is powerful; it will pull down the mighty fortresses and strongholds of lies and deception that demons and men have erected against us.

Second Chronicles chapter twenty talks about God's people who were in a battle. He told them not to be afraid of the enemy or discouraged because of the impending attack. He said, "The battle is not yours, but God's (v. 15)." They did go to fight against their foe, but they followed God's instructions in order to win. His directions on how to wage the battle were not the typical combat procedures of the day. The same is true in our time. His plan may cause others to mock and scoff at us when we employ the weapons God has given to us because they are strange and unfamiliar to most. But never mind the scoffers, don't hesitate or be restrained, just go ahead and win!

God has equipped the believer with spiritual weapons to utilize when we are assailed. We must consistently use these weapons in our lives and especially in prayer.

# PRAYER

*Lord, thank You that You have given me the weapons that will sustain and protect me. As I pray, I receive Your power which allows me to deal with strongholds in my life. I also receive the supernatural ability to discern when confusion and deception are present. I will use Your battle plan to win in life.*

# DAY 15
# MYSTERIES AND SECRETS

*Call to Me and I will answer you and show you great and mighty things, fenced in and hidden, which you do not know (do not distinguish and recognize, have knowledge of and understand)* (Jeremiah 33:3, AMP).

God has given us a powerful prayer promise through the prophet Jeremiah. He tells us that if we will call upon Him by praying, He will answer us and reveal to us things that are hidden from the believer's common gaze. God will bring illumination in situations that we do not understand, and through this we can gain insight into them, either good or bad. When light comes to veiled or cloaked circumstances, it saves us from unnecessary heartache, pain, and difficulty. God can impart knowledge and bring understanding to us if we take time to pray and hear from Him. I am not indicating we will always understand every situation in our lives, but there is much more insight available to us than what we typically experience!

In Peter's second epistle, he revealed that God has already given us all things that pertain to life and godly living. Therefore, wisdom and revelation to guide us have already been made accessible. But many of us would probably say that we aren't experiencing the manifestation of all the knowledge and discernment that we need in our daily lives. It is through our access to the spiritual world that Christ's provision is retrieved and manifested in the earth. God gives us a key to bring answers into our world: praying in faith and receiving a spiritual ear to hear His voice. When we cooperate, He will be able to bring to us clear information and guidance.

Life is filled with intersections where we have to decide which way to go. The Lord tells us to call on Him, and He will give us wisdom and revelation in what we should do. Proverbs says the steps of a man who serves God are ordered and directed by the Lord. If we enter into fellowship with our Creator, we can pray and receive instruction from Him. We then take a step by faith and the Lord will uphold us. He promises to reveal things that are obscured to our casual observation. It is not a common thing for most people to seek God for enlightenment and insight into the unseen realm to help them accomplish a desired result. As a matter of fact, I believe it is very uncommon. Let us make it a point to change this.

When we stay in communication with our heavenly Father, there will be times when He will witness to or impress upon our spirits through the Holy Spirit to pause, stop, or change direction. On the surface, everything may appear to be fine, but the Lord has all knowledge as He sees the end from the beginning. It behooves us to pay attention and listen to the inward voice as we pray. When we listen to His voice He can reveal hidden dangers, obstacles, and traps that the enemy has placed in our path to cause us to stumble or bring trouble into our lives. We don't have to be afraid or alarmed concerning what is revealed to us. The Holy Spirit's voice will impart peace into our hearts. God wants us to be prepared and even prevent many situations that could arise in our lives or the lives of others. If we continually reject or discount the promptings of the Holy Spirit, we will become dull in our ability to discern His voice in our lives.

God does not only give us insight for protection, but He can also give us glimpses into our future as He reveals great and remarkable things to us. God has a good plan for your life, but sometimes a person may never learn or discover that favorable plan. Allow the heavenly Father, in your personal prayer time, to unfold marvelous information to you about your own life. Call upon the Lord and He most assuredly will answer you!

# PRAYER

*Lord, thank You that as I call upon You in prayer that You hear me, You answer me, and You show me things I cannot detect or see on my own. Thank You for insight, wisdom, and understanding for my daily life. In this natural world, I receive the ability to be led by You supernaturally.*

# DAY 16
# FOR OTHERS

*And the men turned their faces from thence, and went toward Sodom: but Abraham stood yet before the Lord. And Abraham drew near, and said, Wilt thou also destroy the righteous with the wicked?* (Genesis 18:22-23).

In this passage of Scripture, Abraham goes before his friend, God, on behalf of his family member, Lot. Standing before the Lord means that Abraham was praying and talking to God—interceding for Lot and his family—because he did not want them to be killed in the coming destruction of Sodom and Gomorrah. This indicates to us that our prayers should not only be about our own lives and needs, but that we should pray for our loved ones and others in our sphere of influence. We should care about them and what they are facing in life. When we see a loved one or someone we know who is in trouble, we should take time to go to the Lord in prayer and intercede for them.

Notice how Abraham "drew near to God."
It is in prayer that we also draw near to Him.
Many people are apprehensive when entering
into God's presence because they feel they are
inadequate or have failed in some way. If He
were looking for perfection before hearing
someone in prayer, He would not be able to listen
to any of us. That is why we need to appropriate
the blood of Jesus Christ and the name of Jesus,
for it is the cleansing power of His blood that
gives us access to God in prayer, and it is His
name that has secured our position in prayer.
When we sin, we can confess it and be forgiven
and cleansed through this precious blood (1 John
1:9). Then, we may go boldly before the throne
of grace in our time of need or we can intercede
on behalf of others without a guilty conscience.
This is where we find help and assistance from
the Lord (Hebrews 4:16).

We do not have to approach Him timidly,
as someone condemned. When we are asking,
seeking, and knocking as a friend of God and intercessor for someone else, God is pleased that
we care enough to pray and act as a go-between
for them. We can enter His presence reverently
and confidently with assurance.

It takes faith and boldness to come to God
and say, "God, this is what You said in Your
Word. I might not be the perfect Christian, but
You are the perfect Redeemer. I believe it's Your
heart for me to pray and intercede for others."

We need to follow Abraham's example of intercessory prayer and come fearlessly into God's presence on behalf of others. The prophet Moses also became an intercessor on behalf of the Israelites and asked God to forgive and help them. Many times the Israelites, in our eyes, may not have deserved it, but Moses prayed and interceded for them anyway. This is another good example for us as intercessors. We can extend God's patience, love, and compassion through our prayers even when people are seemingly undeserving. Many times, people in precarious situations do not sense or detect the ominous signs of danger to their lives, but God has given us a way and means of stepping in for them and making a difference through prayer.

# PRAYER

*Lord, help me to live a pure, clean life so that I am not apprehensive about drawing near to You. Thank You for cleansing and forgiving me when I do sin. I am determined to come boldly before the throne of grace for myself and others. Help me to be cognizant of the needs of those around me and not dismiss their cause, but pray for them.*

# DAY 17
# OUR LEADERS

*I exhort therefore, that first of all, supplications, prayers, intercessions, and giving of thanks, be made for all men; for kings, and for all that are in authority; that we may lead a quiet and peaceable life in all godliness and honesty. For this is good and acceptable in the sight of God our Saviour* (1 Timothy 2:1-3).

In these verses the Apostle Paul is clarifying what types of prayers believers should pray, as well as, for whom we should be praying.

A **prayer of supplication** indicates a petition for a specific purpose and it conveys our humble dependence upon the Lord to meet our needs. *Prayers* here are more general than supplications. Prayers include wishes and desires that we bring before Him in prayer.

**Intercession** is when we pray on behalf of someone else. Moses interceded for the children of Israel, Abraham interceded for Lot when he was in Sodom, and Jesus is our Great Intercessor who prays to the Father for us (1 Timothy 2:5).

**Thanksgiving** is simply being grateful and expressing that gratitude. As believers, we should proclaim our thanks to God daily. If you think you do not have anything to be thankful for in life because of difficulties you may be facing, just spend a few moments thinking of God's mercy, grace, salvation, and where He has brought you from. You will find you have a great deal to be thankful for in spite of these problems.

Paul exhorts us to pray for *kings* or *presidents* and all who are in *authority* that we may lead a quiet and peaceful life. We need to pray for those who are in leadership positions to make right judgments. If there are ungodly leaders in authority, we need to pray that God will replace them with those who will make wise, correct, godly decisions. When peace prevails in a nation the Gospel of Jesus Christ can be preached, but when chaos, upheaval, and war are present, it's very difficult to spread the Gospel. That is why this Scripture and prayer principle should be paramount in our thinking in these last days.

Leaders in all realms need wisdom and discernment, whether spiritual, governmental, occupational, or any other kind of leader. If unsuitable people surround leaders and give unwise counsel, many will suffer the consequences if it is followed; conversely, the right counsel given to a leader at the proper time will bring blessing and benefit into the lives of those affected by their leadership. As you can see, praying for leaders in all realms is vital for a nation or a group. If we don't think what is happening is right, we can pray for the leaders and ask for God's divine intervention into the situation and believe for godly change however it may come.

# PRAYER

*Lord, thank You that You have made many types of prayer available to me. I purpose to pray for my spiritual leaders, for leaders in government and for others in authority. May we have peaceful surroundings where the Gospel can be preached and individuals have an atmosphere to receive Jesus Christ.*

# DAY 18
# FEAR TO FAITH

*"Do not fret or have any anxiety about anything, but in every circumstance and in everything, by prayer and petition (definite requests), with thanksgiving, continue to make your wants known to God"*
(Philippians 4:6, AMP).

God has a recipe for prayer: don't worry—pray; have definite requests. Afterwards, keep thanking Him for the answer to that request. A definite request is a formal written request; God is serious about this prayer business and expects us to be, also.

Anxiety and fear neutralize your faith in God's ability to answer your petition. Because of this, we are instructed not to allow these enemies of our faith to be active in our lives. The Scripture then tells us what to do in place of worry—to pray by making definite requests for our needs that may be wearing us down and then to cast or roll those cares on Him (1 Peter 5:7). To *cast our care* means to hurl it away from our lives and give it to the Lord. As humans, we are unable to handle or deal with great burdens. They will destroy us physically, emotionally, and spiritually. God has provided a way of escape from life's heavy load. As we give it to Him, He will lift the weight of the cares of this life from us.

Thankfulness is an essential attitude when we petition God in prayer. How would you feel if you put a lot of thought into purchasing a very special gift for someone, but then when you presented them with the gift they responded with a nonchalant, "I'll look at it later"? You would probably feel hurt and slighted by that person's lack of appreciation. How often has God done special things for us and we respond with an indifferent, unappreciative attitude? We need to be thankful to the Lord for the many things He does for us by acknowledging His blessings and favor in our lives.

This Scripture from the book of Philippians reveals what we are to do after we initially make our prayer petition to the Lord. In the future, when we reference this request, it should be by thanking Him for hearing us WHEN we prayed the first time and for answering us. We don't have to ask Him repeatedly. Thanking Him for the answer before it is manifested demonstrates our faith in God's ability to provide the answer. We must believe we receive when we petition Him, and then thank Him for it (Mark 11:24).

Philippians 4:7 instructs us to allow God's peace to arrest the devil from the torment he brings into our lives. After we pray, we should not allow an agitating spirit to harass us by telling us, "He didn't hear you; nothing is going to change." Resist and refuse that spirit, and allow the peace of God to dwell in your heart and mind through faith in Christ Jesus. Philippians 4:8 says:

> *Finally, brethren, whatsoever things are true, whatsoever things are honest, whatsoever things are just, whatsoever things are pure, whatsoever things are lovely, whatsoever things are of good report; if there be any virtue, and if there be any praise, think on these things.*

This verse instructs us on how to receive this peace in our heart and mind: by controlling what we think upon. Not meditating on the problem or fears, but meditating on His love, His Word, and His provision for us.

Another part of God's recipe for prayer is to reprogram our minds with the Word of God. Romans 12:2 in the Phillip's translation says, "Don't let the world around you squeeze you into its mold, but let God remake you so your whole attitude of mind is changed." We must update or change our way of thinking. Perhaps you have been a worrier. Through this day of study, you have learned that you should give your cares to Him because you don't have the ability to bear up under them. Then, your thinking can be transformed to allow the Word of God to control your thought processes instead of the cares of this life. Push out the old way of thinking (what has been normal in the past) and allow God's new way to prevail—don't worry, ask and then give Him thanks when you bring it before Him afterwards; break out of the mold the world may have squeezed you into.

# PRAYER

*Lord, help me to put aside my fears and anxieties in each situation and trust You with all my heart. As I am in your presence, I receive Your peace by faith. Thank You for the peace that surpasses all human comprehension. I do believe I receive answers WHEN I pray.*

72

# DAY 19
# MOST POWERFUL NAME

*"And in that day ye shall ask me nothing. Verily,
verily, I say unto you, Whatsoever ye shall ask the
Father in my Name, he will give it you"* (John 16:23).

Those powerful words were spoken by
Jesus Christ. His purpose was to teach His disciples that in the future they would not be asking
Him for anything in prayer; instead, they would
be asking the Father and using His name. Jesus,
through His obedience to the Father in His
death, resurrection, and shedding of His own
blood for us, spoiled principalities and powers
and cancelled out their capabilities against us.
He also made a way for a Christian to be able to
confidently approach the heavenly Father
through His name. The name of Jesus is the
greatest name of all. There is power in that name
(Philippians 2:9).

As we pray, we ask our requests in Jesus'
name—the name above every name—the name of

our Redeemer and the name of the One who sits at the right hand of the Father as our intercessor. In that name, we pray to the Father. One day every knee will bow and every tongue confess that Jesus Christ is Lord.

Does this mean that if we didn't know this and we pray to Jesus, instead of praying to the Father, that God would never hear us? I can't say that is true, but to be obedient and assured of answered prayer, we can only go by what the Bible tells us: pray to the Father in Jesus' name. If these are the words of Jesus, why wouldn't we pray as He instructs us? He wants us to be able to receive the things we have need of when we ask the Father in His name.

Through Jesus, our victorious Lord and Savior, we now have access to come boldly before the heavenly Father. Before He made a way for that to happen through the cross, we had no such promise. John 16:24 says to ask so that we can receive answers and then be filled with joy because of it. God delights in answering our prayers and seeing us pleased and blessed. As parents, we are pleased to see our children happy and excited when we've done something for them. How much more with our heavenly Father?

The balance to this is that we are not talking about flippant, frivolous prayers such as asking God for "one of those" and "one of these."

We are talking about the earnest heartfelt desires and needs that we bring to the Father. I will say the Lord is interested even in the small details of our life. If it genuinely concerns us, it concerns Him.

This Scripture tells us whatever we ask the Father in Jesus' name, He will give it to us. This carries with it the thought: if it doesn't exist, He will create it for us. God is not trying to keep things from us, but rather, to get them to us.

The Bible teaches us that obedience to Him is better than sacrificing. Sometimes people can be living in disobedience and wonder why their prayers are not being answered. "If ye be willing and obedient ye shall eat the good of the land," (Isaiah 1:19). Disobedience will hinder your prayers. Also, notice we need to be willing to do what God asks of us with a right attitude and not reluctantly respond. This verse denotes that a willing attitude is equally as important as obeying. Wouldn't you say that, "eating the good of the land," would be getting your prayers answered? I believe so. If we want our prayers to be answered and experience the favor and blessing of God, we need to be obedient to anything the Lord deals with us about and willing to submit to it.

"And whatsoever we ask, we receive of him, because we keep his commandments, and do those things which are pleasing in his sight"

(1 John 3:22). When our heart is to please God, we obey, yield, and conform to His will—which is His Word. Then, we can ask whatever we want and receive an answer from Him.

# PRAYER

*Father, in Jesus' name, I desire to be willing and obedient to You. I purpose to hear and do what I observe from the Scriptures. Then, when I ask You for my needs and desires to be met, I will believe I receive them in the name of Jesus Christ, my Lord.*

# DAY 20
# PERSISTENCE

*"Ask, and it shall be given you; seek, and ye shall find; knock, and it shall be opened unto you:"*
(Matthew 7:7).

What a directive Jesus gave! Ask (crave, desire strongly) and it will be given to you; seek (search) and you will find; knock (be persistent) and it shall be opened to you.

Too often we have prayed half-hearted, ineffective prayers that did not yield any results. I personally do not ask God for things I don't really want or I am not serious about. If we do this, it will weaken our faith because we won't receive an answer. Then, we begin to believe that prayer does not really work. We start thinking that we should not get too excited in believing that God will answer our prayers because after all, "our prayer might not be answered." When we are in that frame of mind, we get exactly what we are believing for: unanswered prayers. But, we are told to be persistent, and we are to grip our faith in God's miraculous ability to provide and we will receive.

Just as there are times in prayer to ask, there are times to seek. Sometimes we do not know God's plan or purpose; it is essential to seek Him in prayer at that time. Jesus gives us the promise that when we go through those times of searching and pursuing in prayer, we will not be disillusioned—we will discover. Also, when we are in need of answers for our lives, we are to go on a quest for His solutions. The Lord doesn't want us to be passive and allow things to continue on and on in our lives, but press in and look for answers to our dilemma. We will find them.

Jesus also tells us that there will be times we will have to knock. Life is not like a game show where the contestants have to guess which door is hiding the desired prize. Jesus tells us to knock and He will open the right door in our lives. He will open doors and close doors that no man can interfere with. To *knock* means we are looking for something that is not readily seen, but hidden from us. Faith and consistent prayer will blast the door open giving us complete access to our answer.

One translation tells us to ask and keep on asking; seek and keep on seeking; knock and keep on knocking. How often do we tell ourselves or others, "I asked and nothing happened? I was seeking and didn't get an answer. I knocked and nothing opened for me." Firstly, we must consider whether or not it is God's best for us. Keep in mind, our petitions and requests must be in line with the Word of God. Secondly, sometimes we are in line with God's will, but the timing is not right for Him to grant us the answer. Trust in God and don't try to reason too much; keep your faith energized and allow God to work His timing in your life. It is faith and patience that inherit God's promises (Hebrews 6:12).

God is faithful when we ask, seek, and knock.

# PRAYER

*Lord, thank You for the privilege of asking, seeking, and knocking through prayer. Help me to keep my faith alive as I seek Your will and answers in my life.*

# DAY 21
# HIS INSTRUMENT

*Thou art my battle ax and weapons of war: for with thee will I break in pieces the nations, and with thee will I destroy kingdoms; and with thee will I break in pieces the horse and his rider; and with thee will I break in pieces the chariot and his rider, (Jeremiah 51:20-21).*

God wants His children to wage war in prayer to implement His will upon the earth. This is because Satan is trying to impose his own will and strategy over God's. Imagine something that seems benign and as simple as prayer, but it produces tremendous power that cooperates dynamically with God's plan to bring it to pass. We are God's instruments of warfare when we enter into our prayer closet and ask for His will to be done. There are also weapons that are made available to Christian's which are not the typical devices of war as we see today: guns, knives, explosives, etc. Second Corinthians 10:3-5 tells us that our weapons are spiritual in nature, and they pull down strongholds the enemy has established—mostly in the minds of people through his deception. Our spiritual artillery is: the Word of God in our mouth, love, faith, and prayer—such as worship and intercession.

When we pray in faith, it can be compared to a spiritual explosive launched against the schemes of the evil unseen world and the power of God is released to overcome them. The angelic forces of God are also commissioned to do battle (Daniel 10:11-14). The Scripture says angels respond to God's Word so when we pray Scripture, angels begin to move on our behalf. Through prayer, God wants us to be an instrument—His "battle ax"—to break down the walls Satan has built to fortify his own plan on the earth, whether in our life or in the lives of others.

Prayer is God's idea and design. Praying in our personal prayer language in the Spirit (in other tongues) is certainly the foremost way I know to be an effective "weapon of war." Romans 8:26 says the Holy Spirit *assists us* or *takes hold with us against* the powers of darkness. He enables us to speak words divinely in a language we do not know or even understand, but precisely speaks to the situations and persons we are praying for. Then God begins to search the hearts of all involved and intercession is made according to the explicit will of God. It is then that all things work together for our good.

Second Corinthians 10:5 tells us to cast down imaginations or thoughts and every lofty thing that exalts itself against God's Word or will. Our minds truly are the battlefield. Because of this, a person of prayer must deal with wrong, contrary, doubting thoughts. Just as Jesus did, we must answer with the Word of God when these "evil" thoughts come to us. We must say, "It is written." We have a spiritual helmet of deliverance given as part of our spiritual armor (Ephesians 6) by which our heads or minds can be covered from the bombardment of the thoughts the devil brings to us.

Thoughts of failure, defeat, and lack do not become activated until you say them or give voice to them (Matthew 6:31). You may recall the story of Israel's twelve spies who were sent into the Promised Land. Earlier, God Himself had said that He had given this land to them as their possession; however, ten of them brought back what the Scripture calls an "evil" report. The reason their report was evil was because they doubted God's own Word and promise to them. They refused His provision and reasoned away His promises. There were two spies, Joshua and Caleb, who refused to think the way of the others, but instead cast down human reasoning and founded their belief in what God had spoken to them. Caleb was referred to as a man with "another spirit." He wasn't like the ten spies; he believed and trusted in what God had spoken to them. Caleb received a reward, and the other spies were defeated and lost their reward. We have to be like Caleb: see the promise, believe God, and wrestle down and defeat demonic strongholds that come in the form of thoughts to overthrow our faith. In this way, again, we are truly God's instrument in striking the scheme of the enemy and praying the promises.

# PRAYER

*Lord, I place myself in Your hands to personally be used by You through prayer to defeat the strategies of the enemy and to bring forth Your plan on the earth, in my life, and in the lives of others.*

# DAY 22
# DIVERSE PRAYER

*Pray at all times (on every occasion, in every season) in the Spirit, with all [manner of] prayer and entreaty. To that end keep alert and watch with strong purpose and perseverance, interceding in behalf of all the saints (God's consecrated people)* (Ephesians 6:18, AMP).

In two of Paul's letters to the church he wrote that believers should be continually in prayer. First Thessalonians 5:17 says, "Pray without ceasing." Does praying at all times and praying without ceasing mean that everywhere we go, we should be praying out loud? The answer is obviously "no."

*Praying at all times* means we should stay in an attitude of prayer. As we go about our daily lives, we should be mindful and quick to pray whenever and wherever we see a need. We can breathe it out to God even if we are in a situation where it is not possible to verbalize, but it's our heart to God's heart. I will be in my car going or coming and see an ambulance, a car accident, a homeless person, or a stray animal, and I will pray. It's as natural as breathing for me to pray over these situations and ask for God's help for people. This also means wherever we see people with needs and whenever we see the devil at work, we are to call on God for help. We are His ambassadors and representatives on this earth. If we don't pray for these individuals, maybe no one else will.

Paul said to pray with all manner of prayer. This means that there are different types of prayer for various needs. One translation actually says to pray with "all different kinds" of prayer. In athletics, there are many kinds of sports that are all played by different rules; the rules that apply to one do not apply to another. This is true with prayer, too. The prayers of faith, petition, supplication, agreement, dedication and consecration, unity, intercession, praise and worship, and praying in the Spirit have specific guidelines. We pray differently concerning these kinds of prayers. This is His design; following His guidelines will bring remarkable results.

I want to highlight *praying in the Spirit*. First Corinthians 14:15 says, "What is it then? I will pray with the spirit, and I will pray with the understanding also: I will sing with the spirit, and I will sing with the understanding also." We are told here that we can pray concerning what we intellectually know, and we can also pray by partnering with the Holy Spirit when we don't know how to pray (Romans 8:26-27). This is when we pray in other tongues. We don't study to learn this language; it is supernaturally received and given to us. First Corinthians 14:2 explains that we are speaking forth divine secrets—things that are hidden which God wants to reveal to us and bring out into the open!

All of this is available through being baptized or filled with the Holy Spirit. When you come to Jesus Christ and accept Him as Savior and Lord, you receive the Holy Spirit. In Acts 19:2, the Ephesian believers are asked, "Have you received the Holy Ghost (baptized or filled) since you believed?" This denotes there is an experience available beyond our accepting Jesus that will make a radical difference. It will empower us to be a bold witness for the cause of Christ as signified throughout the book of Acts.

This experience is available today. I can attest to the fact that it has forever changed my life and given me a power and intimacy with God I never encountered before nor knew was available. Praying in the Spirit is an awesome and powerful kind of prayer which the Father has made available to all believers. Ask and receive for the baptism of the Holy Spirit by faith. Then, receive your personal, devotional prayer language to talk to God and to speak forth mysteries and secrets.

The action of prayer that takes place *on* the earth precedes action that takes place *in* the earth. Do you sometimes wonder why God does not seem to be intervening? Perhaps it is because there is no action of prayer *in* the earth to bring to pass something *on* the earth. Or could it be because we are not following the prayer guidelines found in the Scriptures for us?

# PRAYER

*Lord, stir me to be prayerful at all times. Cause prayer to be as natural as breathing to me. I ask You, through the teacher of the Holy Spirit, to help me be alert and pray with all different manner of prayer You have made available to me. May I be ever filled with the Holy Spirit.*

# DAY 23
# MOTIVES

*"Ye lust, and have not: ye kill, and desire to have, and cannot obtain: ye fight and war, yet ye have not, because ye ask not"* (James 4:2).

*[Or] you do ask [God for them] and yet fail to receive, because you ask with wrong purpose and evil, selfish motives. Your intention is [when you get what you desire] to spend it in sensual pleasures* (James 4:3, AMP).

James is admonishing the Christian believers concerning how to stay on track spiritually in their prayer life. He is also exposing wrong motives as to why God is not granting answers to some prayers.

"Ye lust, and have not." Although the first thing we tend to think of when we see the word *lust* is sexual sin, it is not confined to the sexual realm. Too often, believers want to skim over certain words or directives in the Bible without taking the time to fully understand their meaning. Concerning lust, it is easy to say, "I don't have impure thoughts, so I do not have a problem with lust." However, the truth is when we desire something and persist on getting it in spite of God's plan, we have become lustful. We can desire things that, in and of themselves, are not necessarily sinful. We can want another career, to move to another city, or to hold certain positions, which again by themselves, are not sinful desires. They become lustful desires when we distinctly understand that they are not part of God's will for our lives, yet we insist and persist in having them anyway.

This can happen to us because we see someone else doing or receiving the very thing we desire, and we grow envious of them. The Lord leaves many things up to us to choose, but in other things He has a better plan. In these cases, it is good to remember to be open to hear or discern His voice in receiving directions from the Holy Spirit. I am not indicating we have to live in limbo—never able to make a solid decision or unable to be precise when we pray. We, of course, can be decisive in our prayer requests and move forward and still remain flexible and teachable to the Holy Spirit's promptings.

"Ye kill." As a Christian, we would certainly never kill or murder another person, yet how many times have we "killed" someone with the words of our mouth by gossiping or speaking harshly against them? Remember, Jesus taught about the Pharisees that sins like murder, vengeance, and adultery begin and emanate from motives of the heart. Others around would not be able to detect it at least for a while, but these evil, contaminating sins can be lurking and churning away in the heart of a man. They are toxic. The Pharisees were not displaying these sins outwardly, they were committing sins of the heart and Jesus addressed them. Sometimes we may covet what someone else has or the joy in life they are experiencing to the point that we would try to "kill" their ability to have it. Envy in our lives is dark and ugly; it will deny others of a blessing even though we will never have it ourselves. This is a part of the fight and war that goes on inside a person that James is talking about.

The wars or internal conflicts within us can also come due to our lack of asking God for what we need or want. The Lord tells us in the gospels that He knows what we need before we ask, but goes on to state to ask Him anyway. This is the way of receiving from the kingdom of God.

If we ask for anything in His name, as long as it is in our covenant (the Bible), He will give it to us. How much turmoil could we spare ourselves if we would strive to seek and understand God's plan for our lives, and then simply ask Him for what we want?

# PRAYER

*Lord, help me to have a pure heart and pure motives when I pray. I trust You because You know what is best for me and what I need. May I put away jealousy and envy from my life. Thank you for granting me answers to my prayers through your abundant supply and provision.*

# DAY 24
# OPEN DOOR

*Continue in prayer, and watch in the same with thanksgiving; withal praying also for us, that God would open unto us a door of utterance, to speak the mystery of Christ, for which I am also in bonds* (Colossians 4:2-3).

Paul is exhorting believers to persist in prayer. The word "continue" means *to keep going or to carry on; to not give up; to persevere.* When you don't see a change in a situation you've prayed about, in spite of it—persevere; don't lose heart or get discouraged. We must allow faith in God and His Word to move the mountains as we press forward in our praying.

We should never think, "I have prayed enough about this or that." The Word tells us to proceed in prayer until we experience the manifestation or answer to your prayer. As you persist in talking to the Father about your need, bring it before Him by thanking Him that He heard you, and He is working conditions to your benefit and causing circumstances to line up and obstacles to be moved. Ask God to assist you and reveal to you if there are other details or developments you need to further talk to Him about.

The word "persevere" means *to go on despite obstacles and opposition.* Obstacles stand in the way in our home life, our church, and our work place. They can come in a personal way as distractions, interruptions, or anything that draws our attention away from our purpose of praying in faith. We have to be diligent and persevere to overcome the obstacles which can be perplexing or simple.

I am a "clean freak" so when I pray I go into the room and switch the lights off so my attention is not turned to other things. I had to learn this early in my spiritual walk with the Lord. This seems very minor, but it was tremendously distracting to me. For the most part, I do not consider the time helping and ministering to people as an interruption or distraction. People, of course, are important and are the reason for ministry. We shouldn't push them aside as an intrusion. However, do note if this happens constantly, the devil is probably using these intrusions to undermine you and your fellowship with the Lord. That's why it's important to choose a regular time and place for prayer; you will be less likely to have so many interruptions.

In verse three of Colossians four, the church was told to continue in prayer in order for the work of the ministry to be able to take place. If the devil can bring distractions, interruptions, or strife-filled situations to people in a local church, he can hinder prayer and thereby thwart fruitfulness and effectiveness in that fellowship. We will be drawn aside into conflict and away from prayer that produces results.

We are also to pray that our spiritual leaders would have freedom and opportunity to speak God's revealed truth to enlighten others concerning the gospel. People and geographical areas are held captive many times because believers are not constant in prayer. A truth may need to be brought forth, but is hindered by the prayerlessness of God's people.

When we earnestly pray we are pressing into the Spirit of God. Let us continue, persevere and push forward despite the obstacles.

# PRAYER

*Lord, I purpose to pray for my spiritual leaders to be fruitful in the ministry inside the church and in the community. May revelation come forth to powerfully communicate the mystery of Christ. Through prayer, may my life be used to touch and bless others.*

# DAY 25
# JESUS' EXAMPLE

*"And it came to pass, that as he was praying in a certain place, when he ceased, one of his disciples said unto him, Lord, teach us to pray, as John also taught his disciples"* (Luke 11:1).

When you look at Jesus' life, you will see that there were many times He withdrew from the hustle and bustle of life and the crowds of people to pray. We need to follow Jesus' example by stealing away in prayer on a consistent basis. We can get caught up in the cares of life and become distracted and unable to genuinely spend time with the Lord in prayer. I call this "fatal distraction" for without God's divine intervention in the affairs of our lives, it is truly lethal.

Many years ago, I learned an important lesson about how distractions that seem so harmless can rob and steal from us. I would get up each morning in the early days of ministry and go to my place of prayer in my home. We also had our church office in our home. As I would begin to pray, there would be diversions to interrupt my time with the Lord, such as pointing out I needed to dust the furniture, vacuum, replace a light bulb, or I needed to call someone and on and on. **My secret in prayer now is to keep a note pad near me and write down a thought, idea or something I need to do.** It's amazing after I come out of my prayer time and look at the list, many of these things are only distractions, and they are not important to me after all. The note taking helps me to leave the thought on paper and continue praying – knowing that if it is important I won't forget it, but will be prompted later.

Notice how Jesus was praying in a *certain place*. Did you know that the Lord wants us to have our own private place in which to pray? Have you ever moved into a new home and found that it took you a little while to find a place for all your furniture and personal things? But once you settle in, you're able to function better because you have a designated spot for everything you need. In the same way, we have to find a place for prayer that fits us. If you have children, you may need to arrange your schedule to have times of privacy even if you have that quiet place. Prayer can become infrequent when you do not have that certain area where you like to go and spend time with the Lord. This is why we need a quiet and secluded place, away from family activities. A place where we know we'll have privacy. We can, of course, pray any time in any place, but we all need this very private place to spend time with the heavenly Father. I am not indicating that you should neglect your spouse or children. Do make time for them, but have your time and place with God, also. I want to add: don't condemn yourself when it doesn't work out the way you planned. Just pick back up the next day and continue on. A red flag should go off in our spirit if we go long periods of time without pulling aside in prayer to be with the Lord.

One place Jesus went to pray was the Garden of Gethsemane. Consider the parallel between Jesus and Adam. In the Garden of Eden, the devil came to Adam and deceived him which resulted in a broken covenant between God and all men. Jesus prayed in the Garden of Gethsemane and the devil came to tempt Him. The garden, in this case, is where Jesus submitted His will to the Father for regaining the redemption of mankind that was lost by Adam and He overcame Satan's temptation. In a real sense, Jesus had to **pray** the price before He could **pay** the price.

There are times when God has something special or new for us, but we do not receive it because we do not pay the price to hear His voice in prayer. We are not paying the price for our redemption—only Jesus could do that; however, we are paying the price to enter into that sweet place of God's presence as He prepares us for what He wants to do in our lives and our futures.

99

Evidently the disciples saw something powerful happen through the prayer life of Jesus. After He prayed, He went forth and did mighty works under the unction of the Holy Spirit. I am sure these men were stirred by the power they experienced working though Jesus' life, because the disciples pleaded, "Lord, teach us to pray." Our desire should be the same: *Lord, teach me to pray so I can do the works You did and experience lives being changed for Your honor and glory.*

# PRAYER

*Lord, I determine in my heart to have a specific time and place to pray as much as possible. I also make a decision to pull away from my daily routine in order to spend time with You. Thank You for times of refreshing which come from being in Your presence.*

# DAY 26
# DISCERNMENT

*"Prepare the table, watch in the watchtower, eat, drink: arise, ye princes, and anoint the shield. For thus hath the Lord said unto me, Go, set a watchman, let him declare what he seeth"* (Isaiah 21:5-6).

At first reading, this seems strange unrelated, and irrelevant, but there is great insight into the subject of prayer in Isaiah chapter twenty-one. The watchtower was a tower on the city wall where a person would go to peer over the surrounding land to be aware of any predators near the city. God wants us to have a position in prayer that is our watchtower; a place in prayer where we are allowed by the Holy Spirit to peer into the unseen realm around us and sound the alarm, if you will, when harm is near.

As we fellowship with God in prayer, it is our chance to mount the city walls and faithfully patrol for enemies that would come against our own life and the lives of others. The enemy desires to set snares or traps for us that are deceitfully camouflaged. As we come to God in prayer, He can and will show us things before they come to pass. Many times, we can pray hindrances out of the way. He will reveal things to us by the Spirit—divine secrets and mysteries. This manner of prayer lends itself to being an intercessor for the needs of others. Jeremiah 33:3 says, "Call unto me, and I will answer thee, and shew thee great and mighty things, which thou knowest not." God will most assuredly answer our prayer when we come to Him. The mighty things are things that have escaped the normal vision of most; this again demonstrates that God will give us insight into His secrets in times of praying.

Does this mean that God will always show us everything concerning our lives or the lives of our loved ones? Of course not; although God does not reveal all things, He will reveal some things so we can stand against them in prayer to thwart the plan of the enemy before it comes to pass. Also, I've learned in my own life that there are things I am not ready to hear; I couldn't deal with them. Being in prayer—talking to the Lord—is one place to have this information disclosed. If there is no watchtower, no continuance in prayer, and no divine connection through prayer, there will be times we experience things that could have been avoided had we sought the Lord.

Notice, He said to anoint the shield. In former days of battle, the soldiers stretched animal skins over their shields. In order to keep the skins from drying out and becoming combustible, the soldiers would saturate them with oil. A saturated shield would protect the soldier from the flaming arrows of the enemy. A dry shield would easily catch fire and diminish its protective ability. In the book of Ephesians, Paul instructed us to put on the whole armor of God, including the shield of faith that would quench all the fiery darts of the enemy. We know that oil represents the Holy Spirit. Therefore, when we pray, our shield of faith can be saturated by the Holy Spirit to stop and extinguish the fiery arrows of the enemy.

Enter into your watchtower of prayer, brandish the shield of faith. Allow the Father to show you the concealed things. Declare what you see, and ask for God's help. It isn't enough just to see something coming, we must declare it. Proclaim that God is greater than troubles, difficulties, and catastrophes. Declare that He has destroyed Satan's power through Jesus' blood and name. Declare God's plan if He has revealed it to you in a time of prayer, or declare what the Scriptures say in a situation like yours. Speaking forth in faith what is revealed to us in prayer is tremendously powerful and changes circumstances. It is utilizing supernatural ability to retrieve the answers on the earth from the spiritual kingdom.

# PRAYER

*Lord, I take my position in prayer. I determine to keep my faith alive and growing. I allow the anointing of the Holy Spirit to lead, guide, and protect me. I will declare what You show me to thwart the plans of the enemy and bring Your purposes to pass. I will be Your watchman.*

# DAY 27
# KEYS

*And I will give unto thee the keys of the kingdom of heaven: and whatsoever thou shalt bind on earth shall be bound in heaven: and whatsoever thou shalt loose on earth shall be loosed in heaven* (Matthew 16:19).

One of the ways that we, as believers, are going to stop the gates of hell and the power of darkness from overwhelming us is by going forward on the offensive in prayer using the keys of the Kingdom that have been given to us by God. As a Christian and a person of prayer, there are times we need to obtain the key at the right time and in the right situation in order to disallow conditions that may be happening around us. Circumstances can be changed when we, in our prayer time, constrict the enemy's authority and loose God's mighty wonder-working power. When praying in this way, we use the name of Jesus because Jesus defeated principalities and powers and gave us the authority, through His name, to forbid the enemy's encroachment (Philippians 2:9-10).

The times we live in are filled with ungodliness, corruption, filth, and perversion. We, as dedicated people of prayer, can intervene in our world and allow God to make a difference through our lives. We cannot stand idly by and tolerate wickedness and evil. The Lord has given us the responsibility to step in and change the affairs of life by praying. We should be concerned about what concerns Him. Because of this, we shouldn't consent to apathy and indifference taking root in our lives. *Apathy* is a lack or absence of passion and enthusiasm for the things of God, and when it sets in, effective prayer is out. We can fight this apathetic fog by communing with the Father through Scripture (Him talking to us), prayer (us talking to Him), and listening for the still, small voice of the Holy Spirit.

The Amplified Bible says it like this: "...and whatever you bind (declare to be improper and unlawful) on earth must be what is already bound in heaven." We must take what God has already declared as unlawful in the Scriptures and agree with it, cooperate with it, and speak His Word in our praying. We cannot have our own rules and regulations. If God has declared something to be unlawful, we must take the key of the Kingdom—prayer—and enforce what He has said. When we speak out of our own mouths what He has already declared, angels listen and are activated on our behalf (Psalm 103:20). In turn, God's will is done on the earth.

The converse is true, as well. If God has declared something to be lawful and proper, we must take this key of the Kingdom and enforce it through our prayers. Just because God has said it should be, doesn't mean that the devil will not fight against it. Decide to be God's enforcer with your life—pray to allow and pray to disallow. In a real way, we are partnering with the God of heaven to bring His will into the earth.

# PRAYER

*Lord, thank You for the redeeming life of the Lord Jesus Christ. Jesus defeated death, hell, and the grave and He gave me the keys of His Kingdom. I accept and receive this power to bind and to loose. Help me to understand Your principles so I can be in agreement with Your Word to implement Your covenant on the earth. Help me not to turn a blind eye towards injustice and ungodliness which seek to prevail around me.*

# DAY 28
# PRETENSE OR GENUINE

*And when you pray, you shall not be like the hypocrites. For they love to pray standing in the synagogues and on the corners of the streets, that they may be seen by men. Assuredly, I say to you they have their reward* (Matthew 6:5, NKJV).

Prayer should be earnest, heartfelt communication between us and our heavenly Father. Jesus Himself had a great deal to say about this subject and did so by teaching the disciples many principles of prayer. He took time to answer their questions regarding prayer because He wanted them to understand there are correct ways and incorrect ways to receive that will hinder our desired outcome.

This may be shocking to some, but God does not receive all of our prayers. Jesus rebuked certain people in the Bible who demonstrated the wrong attitude concerning prayer by obnoxiously praying publicly so others would notice and pay attention to them. He refers to these people as hypocrites. They would try to impress those around them by their eloquent words or pitiful demeanor. All this didn't move our Lord. What moves Him is a sincere heart crying out to God in faith to believe that He can affect a change for them.

Is Jesus telling us that we should not pray in public? No. There are many examples in the Bible where people publicly assembled together and prayer was made. Is Jesus telling us to pray silently so that no one else will hear us? No. There are many examples of believers gathering together and everyone lifting up their voices out loud in united prayer all at the same time.

Jesus was teaching us that when we pray, we should always pray with pure motives and honest intentions. There were people in Jesus' time, and there are people now, who like to pray in order to get praise of men and recognition for how spiritual they are because of the impressive prayer that they prayed.

Jesus strictly warns us that prayers with prideful intentions will receive no reward or answer from heaven. These types of prayers receive their just reward, which are the accolades of men. They may impress human beings, but it's help from the Creator God that is needed to change our circumstances. The Lord is not inspired by our intelligence or presentations. He is moved by our faith in Him. This will open the heavens and bring answers to Earth.

We all want and need our requests to be heard and answered. Our objective should never be to impress others or attempt to impress God. How could we ever impress Him? He is almighty, infinite, and all-knowing, and we are only finite beings with a human perspective. He, again, expects genuine, heartfelt prayers with right intentions so that answers can be given. The desire of the Father is to reward and bless His children when we seek Him. He is not endeavoring to complicate prayer, but simplify and point out hindrances to receiving answers to our prayers.

# PRAYER

*Lord, teach me to pray. Disclose to me wrong motives and intentions in my heart. Help me desire to be pleasing to You and not try to impress others.*

# DAY 29
# THE HARVEST

*"Pray ye therefore the Lord of the harvest, that he will send forth labourers into his harvest"* (Matthew 9:38).

One of our roles or duties as people of prayer is to ask God to send forth believers to go into the world to touch the lives of those who need to accept Jesus Christ. We are to pray for individuals to come into the Kingdom of God by being born again. We know that even as we pray for the workers to go to our loved ones, we will also be called upon by God to go to the loved ones of someone else who, like us, is praying.

Churches and individuals in those churches that do not pray for people to come to know the Lord are not in the will of God. He commands us to pray so laborers will go forth. God does not want anyone to perish; His desire is for all to come to the saving knowledge of the Lord Jesus Christ. A Christian's responsibility is to not be neglectful in this kind of praying.

It is a sobering thought to realize that people may not come to God if we do not pray for them. Many times, individuals do not receive the Lord because the god of this world (Satan) has blinded their minds (2 Corinthians 4:3-4). The truth is veiled or cloaked from them and they are deceived. Once the blindfold is removed from those who do not believe, the illumination of God's Word will bring revelation of the truth. They will be able to realize that they are lost or unsaved and that they are actually living under the curse of hell from which Jesus redeemed them.

Once the blinders are off and the light breaks through, they will realize their need for a Savior. Their hearts will become tender toward God, and they will be open to accept Jesus Christ as their Lord.

In the New Testament, Jude talks about snatching people from the fires of hell. I believe this is done, to a large degree, by praying for individuals to have an opportunity to receive Jesus Christ. The choosing of these individuals is determined in our prayer closet when we mention specific names to the Lord and ask God to send someone to share the Gospel with them. This is a sobering assignment that we have. May we all take it seriously.

Jesus Christ went to Calvary to redeem us from the curse of the law (Galatians 3). This curse consists of sickness, poverty, and hell. You can read more about the curse in Deuteronomy 28. God wants all of us to not be deceived and blinded from the truth, but to receive light, revelation, and deliverance from eternal judgment. We, as Christians, must maintain a compassion for the unsaved—that's the heart of God. We must continually pray for the laborers and for the harvest to come in; then, be open to God to be used as the one He sends to present the Good News of the Gospel.

# PRAYER

*Lord, help me to not neglect to pray for those who need Jesus Christ. May I maintain a compassion for the lost and intercede for them regularly. Help me to not only pray, but be willing to go into all the world and share my faith with others.*

# DAY 30
# UNITED

*"And said unto them, It is written, My house shall be called the house of prayer; but ye have made it a den of thieves"* (Matthew 21:13).

When this true story took place, Jesus was upset and grieved by what was happening in the temple—God's house. People were using the temple for their own selfish gain, rather than coming to worship God and pray to Him for their needs and the needs of others. They were caught up in all the wrong things—sidetracked by their self-centeredness, greed, and lack of concern for spiritual matters.

We can have so-called "prayer meetings" in our churches and barely spend time praying at all; yet, prayer in church is the very heart of God. His house is to be known for the praying that takes place there. Earth-shaking prayers can come forth as Christians unite together as they did in the book of Acts. Just as it was in the early church, when they prayed and power was released; lives were changed, unbelievers believed, and Satan was unable to stop God's people—so it can be in our time. We can turn the world upside down for the Gospel. But, this will not take place by believers being passive and playing the church game. It will happen when God's people earnestly and humbly pray in the ways God has disclosed to us.

I believe spiritually blind eyes can be opened, hearts can be softened, and lives remarkably changed through this simple, but profound truth of prayer. I learned a Latin phrase a French monk coined many centuries ago that has remained with me through the years. It is "ora labora," which means *pray and work.* As humans, we have a tendency to work and work until we are utterly exhausted, and then as a last resort— pray. This monk learned to pray first. We need to understand this valuable truth, and then we will be better able to handle the process ahead of us because we have sought God FIRST. Let's work smarter through prayer, not harder.

When we go to church, we go to worship and seek God for our own lives. Worship is the lifting of hands, bowing of knees, and having a voice of praise and thanksgiving. This is a form of prayer. Also, our heavenly Father wants us to come to Him on behalf of others and not become self-centered. We should pray in our homes, of

course, but God's house—the local church—
should most definitely be a place where we unite
with other believers and make our requests
known to the Lord, as well as intercede for
others.

If we update our mindset concerning the
local church as being a place of prayer, I believe,
it will evoke hope, courage, strength, and greater
faith in our hearts and bring the same to others.
For when we go to our church, we will expect
God to meet us in the miraculous power of the
Holy Spirit.

# PRAYER

*Lord, I make a decision that my church is a house of prayer. I will participate, support, and unite with other believers in prayer to make it fully realized. Help me to remember to pray to You first, before I begin my endeavors.*

# THE MOST
# IMPORTANT PRAYER

## Prayer of Salvation

If you have never made Jesus Christ the Lord of your life or if you have strayed from your relationship with Him, today is your day. You can pray the greatest prayer of all—asking Jesus to come into your heart and be your Lord and Savior. If you pray this prayer and mean it, you can have eternal life and become a "new creation" as the Bible says.

*Father, I come to You in the Name of Jesus. I believe Jesus died on the cross and shed His blood for the cleansing and forgiveness of my sin and was raised from the dead.*

*Jesus, I ask You to come into my heart. I accept You as my Lord and Savior. I will live for You and serve You all the days of my life. Take my life and use me for Your honor and glory.*

Now that you have prayed and asked Jesus to come into your life:

- Share with someone that you accepted Jesus Christ.
- Read the Bible daily. Start with the book of John and go forward.
- Pray daily.
- Find a Bible-based church where you can worship and get involved.

**Welcome to the "family"!**

# ABOUT THE AUTHOR

Nora King was born and raised in Knoxville, a city located near the Smoky Mountains of East Tennessee. She grew up the second of four children and her father, a Baptist preacher, set a godly example for her, teaching her to love and serve the Lord. She came to Jesus Christ at the age of thirteen, but never really lived for God until years later when she attended a Billy Graham Crusade and re-dedicated her life to Jesus Christ. From that experience, Nora began to learn more about the Lord as she read the Bible completely for the first time and discovered truths that changed her life in a profound way.

She married her high school sweetheart, Ed. Their family grew with the birth of their daughter, Laren, followed by their son, Marcus.

Early on, her husband felt God leading him into the ministry. Being brought up as a "preacher's kid," Nora knew the hardships and challenges that she and her husband would face, but they wanted to follow God's path for their lives. Together they took a step of faith. Nora helped her husband establish a church while continuing to be a devoted mother.

During that time, Nora was sitting alone watching a minister on television late one Sunday evening when she felt the Holy Spirit speak clearly to her, calling her to preach. She answered the call and was ordained into ministry by Dr. Lester Sumrall. Nora and her husband also had the opportunity to be a part of a small group of young pastors who traveled around the world with Dr. Sumrall, gaining valuable experience from his anointed ministry. She went on to earn a Bachelor of Arts in Theology from Zoe University and has pursued the study of Christian and secular leadership principles.

Nora has experienced difficult, painful, and challenging circumstances in her life, but she learned to trust, depend, and lean upon God and has always found Him to be faithful. It was through the ever-evolving process of seeking and knowing God through His Word that Nora began exploring the depths of prayer. As she spent time in God's presence, her passion and fervency grew. She was drawn into a more intimate relationship with Him and began to experience prayer on a deeper level. She has seen the effects of the power of prayer resonate throughout her life and ministry. She not only learned about the promises of God and what He is able to do, but she learned how to unlock the secrets and mysteries to actually receive from Him and acquire what He has in store for her life.

She discovered that powerful and fruitful prayer is not complicated or difficult, and has shared these "prayer secrets" countless times through the years in prayer meetings and church services. She has traveled throughout the world ministering God's Word with boldness and compassion and hearts are stirred, provoked, and changed by the power of the Holy Spirit.

Today, Ed and Nora continue to work together as a ministry team. Nora co-pastors the church she helped her husband start thirty years ago. She has cultivated and maintains the volunteer ministry teams of the church, which includes mentoring and teaching leadership and developing procedural training manuals. Her oversight includes the church staff and pastoral care. Her daughter, Laren, works alongside her mom and dad in the ministry.

### The Curse Reversed – CD series

Many people don't realize that when they receive Jesus as their Savior, they have access to everything that He came to redeem us from. Sickness, poverty, and the lack of peace in your life are all part of the curse. Christ came to redeem us from the curse of the law. Be encouraged to study the Scriptures to find out what truly belongs to you.

### Building A Healthy Self-Image – CD series

Wouldn't it be wonderful if "sticks and stones may break your bones, but words can never hurt you" was true? Words really do pierce our heart and many times stay with us for years. Learn how to shut out verbal, negative input and understand what the Word of God says about you. Listen as Pastor Nora King teaches you how to see yourself in the mirror of God's Word!

### Untied & Free – CD series

The enemy wants to bind and restrict, but Jesus wants to set you free. You don't have to live restrained and bound. Storms of life do come, but you will not be moved if your house has a solid foundation. This powerful series can help you gain freedom in every area of your life!

### Faith Booster – CD series

When you begin to feel the heat from the pressures of life, the Lord doesn't want you to grow weary or give-up. He says that the man who trusts and has confidence in Him will have provision. Listen to these messages by Pastor Nora King and BOOST YOUR FAITH to the next level.

### End Time Faith – CD series

With great passion, Pastor Nora King gives Christians a wake-up call that the time for faith is now! In this series, she not only gives reasons why we need to be growing in faith, but she also shows you ways to do it.

### Forgive & Choose to Forget - CD series

When Peter asked Jesus how many times he should forgive someone, Jesus responded 490 times a day, or in other words, as many times as it takes. Forgiveness frees you from bitterness. This teaching will help you learn to forgive and choose to forget so you can be free to enjoy life as God intended.

### Take Your Seat - CD series

Anytime you attend a special dinner where dignitaries are present, there will be a seating arrangement already prepared. Jesus gives you placement at His side. You may have feelings of unworthiness, but He pulls out a chair for

you and says, "I saved you a seat." Pastor Nora teaches you how to overcome your feelings of inferiority and insecurity and shows you how you can take your position in Christ.

### The School of Prayer - CD series

There is power in prayer. It can affect history, world events, and your own destiny. People who pray and intercede in prayer are enforcers of God's will on the earth. In this enlightening and informative series you can learn how to have a more effective personal prayer life. Pastor Nora explores the principles on prayer found in the Bible and shows you how to apply them to your life.

# BOOKS BY DR. ED KING

### How to Be Twice As Happy

Are you happy? When everything goes according to plan...when everything works exactly like we want it to...when life is good, it's easy to be happy. Life, however, can and does throw many things our way that cause our happiness quotient to decrease dramatically. In this book Dr. King shares twenty important keys to true happiness.

### Cause & Effect:
### Staying Free From the Curse

Jesus redeemed us from the curse of the law. Dr. King teaches you how to stay free from the curse of the law and live in God's blessings.

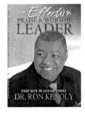 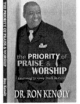

## WITH EVERY BEAT OF MY HEART
### A Weekly Devotional by Jeff North

 Explore real life examples in real Christian living. **With Every Beat of My Heart** takes the reader to a place where inspirational stories and poems stay upon their hearts and lips throughout the day. This book offers a practical message with a godly foundation to encourage, motivate, and bring comfort (224 pages). Order today for only $14.95 + $4 S/H.*

## PORTRAIT OF A PASTOR'S HEART
### A Manual on Caring for the Sheep
### by Bishop Gerald Doggett

This book is a must for pastors, elders, students & laymen who want to learn how to care for the flock of God. Bishop Gerald Doggett paints a rare and intimate portrait of a pastor's heart. He covers TOPICS such as: Spirit of a Finisher, The Necessity of the Divine Call and A Beautiful Portrait of Preparation. Order your copy today for only $12.95 + $4 S/H.*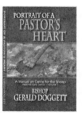

## RELEASE YOUR WORDS - IMPACT YOUR WORLD
### by Darrell Parsons

 Your words can make a difference! God has done something in the life of every believer. He has placed treasures inside you that He wants to use to touch hearts and minds. In this book, Darrell Parsons challenges you to use your voice to impact the world around you today. Order your copy for only $9.95 + $4 S/H.*

## MOUNTAIN VIEW - A Photo Collection
## by Doris Beets

Contained in these pages is a beautiful, color pictorial discovery of a community in East Tennessee where splendor is exemplified and where beauty is personified. In this book, Doris Beets attempts to give you a glimpse of the world that captured her heart over 75 years ago. Only $29.95 + $4 S/H.*

## LIFTING HIM UP
## by Ron Kenoly & Dick Bernal

Worship leader Ron Kenoly teams up with his pastor, Dick Bernal, in this practical guide to praise and worship. You'll learn how to enter into the Lord's presence, plus you'll gain insight into the scriptural role of praise and worship in your life and church. Order your copy today for only $12.95 + $4 S/H.*

## CAPTURING THE HEART OF GOD
## by Diane Parsons

God created man for His good pleasure. Our most satisfying goal should be to bring delight to our heavenly Father. Make it your goal today to do those things which please God. This book contains practical tips on capturing God's heart and becoming His delight everyday. Order your copy for only $10.95 + $4 S/H.*

**\*Shipping Prices for U.S. only.**

# AVAILABLE AT YOUR LOCAL BOOKSTORE

STL | Distribution
North America

I knowledge him
Being with me
Living in me
Being real
Lord I Trust in the
Lord

Direction my path
show the path

LaVergne, TN USA
08 July 2010
188750LV00003B/4/P